Midlife Crisis: An Astrological Approach

Midlife Crisis:

An Astrological Approach

Understand the Timing of Crisis,

Learn How to Turn a Crisis into an Opportunity

Author

Ajay Srivastava

First Edition, 2023

Published by:

Ajay Kumar Srivastava

45, Awas Vikas Colony, Betiya Hata,

Gorakhpur – 273001 (U.P.), India

Mobile No.: +91-9867837184

Disclaimer: This publication contains the opinions and ideas of its author and is designed to provide useful information in regard to the subject matter covered. The author and the publisher specifically disclaim any responsibility for liability, loss, or risk, personal or otherwise, that is incurred as a consequence, directly or indirectly, of the use and application of any of the contents of this book.

Lord Hanuman

Prayer

ॐ आंजनेयाय विद्महे वायुपुत्राय धीमहि |

तन्नोः हनुमत् प्रचोदयात ||

Meaning: O, the son of Anjana and Vayu, please I pray to you for intellect and knowledge.

Dedication

I dedicate this book to my father (Late) Sri R.A.L Srivastava who taught me to be an independent, courageous and determined person, and my mother Maya Srivastava whose unconditional love and support always help me to overcome all the obstacles in my life. She has a selfless spirit and served others throughout her life. Her immense patience is peerless and she always inspires me to go ahead.

Preface

A speeding train changes its track at the junction. When the train approaches the junction, its speed slows down and those who have experienced train travel know that when the train is changing its track the sound of the wheel changes. Junctions are essential for smooth transit of the train and several tracks are necessary to transfer the train from one route to another. Junctions are important to the train system and without which a train cannot cover the long journey.

Human life is such a long journey with various twists and turns. Midlife is the junction from where the track begins to change. The pace does not remain the same and a person starts witnessing disharmony in various aspects of life. Such as stress in career or business, sudden health problems, financial problems, disruption in mutual understanding with partner, etc.

We travel by train many times, so we are aware of such incidents. But during mid-life, when the track in life starts to change and its pace slows down then people are unaware of such incidents. Some of them starts blaming others for such happenings and some start feeling frustrated. They want to maintain the speed at which they have travelled so far, but their subconscious mind does not support the path they have travelled so far. So different kinds of contradictory thoughts start coming in their mind.

Also, a person has different responsibilities at this stage of life. They have family, friends, and other social responsibilities. All of them force them not to change the track and lead a peaceful life. But change has started and many people start witnessing such a change in their daily life. They feel that they cannot ignore their inner voice but it is difficult to change track. So, the stress level becomes very high at this time, every step is important and should be taken with full consideration.

According to astrology, when slow-moving planets start making hard aspects then changes start in life and as life progresses, one has to go through such phases but changes and lessons are different for every person. It depends on what kind of aspects and conjunction the transiting planet is making along with the planets positioned in the birth chart.

Such transits of planets have changed my life forever. I started my career as a research analyst at a leading business news channel and moved on to various profiles on wealth management and investment banking. I was the one who didn't believe in astrology at all. But something has changed during my midlife. I started reading ancient texts and various other books on astrology and soon my collection of books becomes huge.

Suddenly my intense journey started from one city to another city and I started witnessing many other changes in my life. At that time, I was unaware of any such concept of a midlife crisis.

Later, I took admitted to astrology at Bhartiya Vidya Bhavan, Mumbai, and started learning there. One day this topic was discussed in the classroom and I came to know about how planetary forces deeply affect a person's life at such times. I was the one whose life was going through such a transition. Therefore, I started collecting a lot of information. I started having discussions with other individuals who have passed their midlife or are currently going through such phases. I noted down all the results and made some predictions and later they came true.

I observed that many people are unaware of such changes in life and due to the lack of direction they wander here and there. They want their speedy life back but changes are inevitable.

I gathered all my data and decided to write a book that can provide some guidance to those who are looking for some direction at this juncture of life.

I am very grateful to the teachers of Bhartiya Vidya Bhavan, Mumbai, who helped me a lot in clarifying various complex concepts of astrology. I give special thanks to my younger brother Abhay Srivastava for their valuable suggestions, without which such work would not have been possible.

Ajay Srivastava

23rd Aug 2022

Acknowledgement

The existence of this book would not have been possible without the help of my wife Seema and my daughter Saanvi. They provided me enough help to write down my thoughts which I have collected so far in my life. My wife has been instrumental as an illustrator and proof-reader and has given me enough insights to write the matter in a simple and explanatory manner.

Ajay Srivastava

Contents

Chapter 1

Introduction

Human life is divided into different stages. When a person enters puberty full of energy, he starts making various plans about his future. Some of them start their journey at a very early stage in life and some start after wandering here and there but everybody has a plan for their future. After starting the journey, we learn one thing that success requires hard work, and nothing is achieved easily. If we want to go ahead in life, we have to work very hard consistently because this is the only way to achieve success in life.

The journey to explore and win the world begins now. The lessons they learn in their childhood and adolescent age help them to go ahead in life. When the wind turns favorable the journey is pleasant and they keep growing in their life. Although obstacles are part of the journey, but they have a strong will to overcome it.

But life doesn't always go the way we plan. When a person reaches middle age many of them start feeling dissatisfied with their life. The goal they had thought of at the beginning of the journey is far away and the life cycle begins to turn in a different direction. They are smart, hardworking, and intelligent people and they never thought that such a crisis could come in their life and they would be completely caught in the circumstances.

Whatever the lessons they learned till now are not working. Conditions have completely changed and nothing is working. They find that they are completely helpless. Such an outcome at this stage of life is far from their thoughts and it is not even close to their dream.

Many of them start taking depression pills and isolating themselves from their circle of friends and other relationships. The person who once had a very busy schedule now isolates himself in a room. Party lovers also start avoiding all kinds of activities. Many of them start thinking that their career is ruined and they will never rise again in their life, this is the end of the journey.

According to astrology midlife crisis is a phase, but this phase does not come in everyone's life. It affects only those people who have such specific combinations in their horoscope.

I examined various phases of human life on astrological perspective in this book that affect deeply during such time. Chapter 2 of the book examines how a crisis begins in a person's life. Chapter 3 discusses the astrological aspects and Chapter 4 discusses the various causes of depression according to astrology and how to overcome them. I decided not to jump directly on how the transit of planets affect us because the understanding of the characteristics of the planets is necessary without which we cannot understand how such transition will affect us. So, Chapter 5 deals with behavior of planets, and Chapter 6 deals with the transit of planets. Chapters 7 deals with various astrological remedies and Chapter 8 discusses how to turn a crisis into an opportunity. (Note: Some contents and chapters in this book are taken from my book "Vedic Astrology: The Light of Wisdom")

Every crisis inflicts some kind of loss that the person is not ready to accept because it is not happening according to his wish and plan. Midlife crisis is a transition phase and this transition creates a serious impact on the life of the individual. This phase paves the way for a new journey. This transition phase provides an opportunity for the individual to introspect.

Midlife crisis provides an opportunity to re-think your desires and goals in life. At the beginning of the journey, the person is not mature enough but after passing the different stages of life now his eyes are no longer blurry.

Midlife crisis makes a big impact on those who have gone through such phases in life. Crisis creates problems but it also provides opportunities. Therefore, it is good to accept the crisis only then one can identify the opportunity. So, introspect yourself and accept that your life is changing.

Time is not always the same. After some time, when the tide turns, one is ready to enter the battle of life again with such a deep knowledge, which he would not have, if he had not seen such phases in life.

Chapter 2

The Beginning of the Crisis

As per astrology, the midlife crisis occurs between the age of 42 to 49 years. The planetary forces affect this physical body and their transit and aspect on different zodiac signs produces different types of energy. When a person crossed or about to cross the age of 42 years, then these transit starts affecting in a cumulative manner. Transit of five planets (slow-moving planets) viz., Jupiter, Saturn, Rahu, Uranus and Neptune are responsible to create such situation at the middle age of the person.

When 1) Ascendant, 2) MC (Medium Coeli) or 10th house, 3) Sun and 4) Moon are aspected by these slow-moving planets and form conjunction, square or opposition aspects (hard aspects) or when such planets create these aspects to their own natal position then the person's life starts changing after the age of 42 years.

Suddenly, circumstances change drastically with no positive sign at such time. Various incidents start happening at such stage which is beyond control of the person. People do not understand what is happening in their lives. They try very hard to change the circumstances but the result is far from their expectations. They start feeling dissatisfied which gradually convert into frustration and then depression. At the onset of the journey, they feel that at such age of life they will reach at the top but now the reality is totally opposite, rather than reaching on the top suddenly their life hit the bottom. At this stage the turmoil is very forceful and their life is pulling in some other direction which they never thought and their every effort to change the situation goes in vain.

The problem comes one after another and the smooth run towards the sky suddenly disappears. Many of them are not ready to accept such happenings. They are working very hard for years, and suddenly many things have changed.

Astrology says that during such phase all the five planets come together and the cumulative energy of these planets creates tension, struggle, financial loss, or danger to life etc. Problems in midlife are not related to career only, it can be of any type. For some of them their savings may vanish after a series of unpleasant events, some of them may face problem related with the family or any major health issue suddenly occurs, etc.

Human life is a journey and at every stage we learn something. The crisis at middle age is also very important to understand. This is the phase of transition and many of them are not ready to accept it. Life always teaches us a new lesson, circumstances teach us and gradually we improve ourselves with a belief for a consistent, dynamic and bright future.

As the situation become worse because all five planets suddenly catch the person, but they start leaving one after another in transit. Jupiter stays in a sign for one year, Rahu stays in a sign for 1.5 years, Saturn stays in a sign for 2.5 years, Uranus stays in a sign for 7 years and Neptune stays in a sign for almost 14 years. Among them the transit of Saturn, Rahu and Uranus are very important. When these planets start creating hard aspects simultaneously, the person face a lot of tension and struggle in his life. During such phase almost three years of the time teaches a very tough lesson to the person.

Just as the crisis begins, it ends in the same way, but such a period teaches a new lesson to a person in life. Such crises examine who their true friends are and what is the real face of the ones they trusted so much till now.

The condition starts easing when planets start changing their position. As all of them suddenly catch the person, but when their time is over, they start changing their sign and the situation in life also starts easing. Real changes begin to be visible when tough master Saturn changes his position.

Now the phase of dark night has gone and the time of dawn is coming soon. Every planet gives their own signal and easing of the situation indicates that the time is changing again.

Chapter 3

Aspects

Planets not only affect the signs and houses in which they are situated but also influence other zodiac signs and houses. Planetary energy works in geometric shape and when it makes geometrical relation with other points or planets from its position then it starts doing its work which is called aspect in astrology.

Five major planetary aspects are considered in astrology:

1. Conjunction

2. Sextile

3. Square

4. Trine

5. Opposition

Astrology has divided the entire space into 12 equal signs. Each sign has its own element and its own quality. Each planet has its own characteristics and the energy they generate depends on the type of elements they are located in the birth chart and the type of energy they are generating in the transit chart. The combination of these two types of energies affects the life of the person.

The following table shows the name of the zodiac, element, and its quality.

Table 1:

No.	Sign	Element	Quality
1	Aries	Fire	Movable
2	Taurus	Earth	Fixed
3	Gemini	Air	Dual
4	Cancer	Water	Movable
5	Leo	Fire	Fixed
6	Virgo	Earth	Dual
7	Libra	Air	Movable
8	Scorpio	Water	Fixed
9	Sagittarius	Fire	Dual
10	Capricorn	Earth	Movable
11	Aquarius	Air	Fixed
12	Pisces	Water	Dual

The below horoscope represents better the above table.

Chart 1: House, Element, and Quality

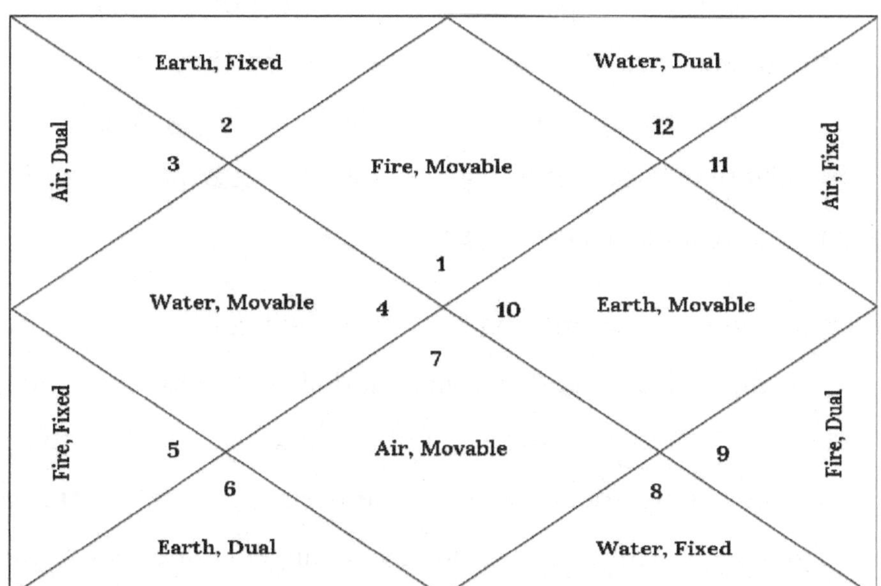

3.1 Conjunction

When two or more planets reach the same sign and do not make any distance between each other, then it is called a conjunction. An orb with a difference of up to 8° is usually regarded as close conjunction, meaning the merging of the energies of two or more planets into a single sign. However, the effect of conjunction for the fast-moving planets begins early and the effect of slow-moving plants begins when the planet comes very close to the other planet i.e., less than 5°. When the planet is about to cross the other planet, its effect is more and when the planet has crossed, its effect becomes less.

How this combination produces results depends on the characteristics of the planets and the element of the zodiac. For example, Sun and Mars are hot planets and they give better results in a fire sign (Aries, Leo and Sagittarius) than any other sign. Whereas Saturn is a dry and cold planet which does not give good results in a fire sign.

Conjunction of slow-moving planets is the beginning of a new cycle in life and it depends on what kind of energies are merging and in which element. If the element of the zodiac and the nature of the merging planets are the same then it generates strong energy which brings various positive changes in life, but if the element does not support the nature of the planets or the nature of merging planets themselves are different then such situation will create chaos and various difficulties in life.

3.2 Sextile

The sextile aspect is considered when two or more planets form an angle of 60° with each other. The planet situated in a fire sign make a sextile aspect with the planets situated in the air sign and so on. This aspect is considered a good aspect and helpful as it supports the other sign. The planets situated here support each other due to the element in which they are situated, even though their nature is opposite.

Chart 2:

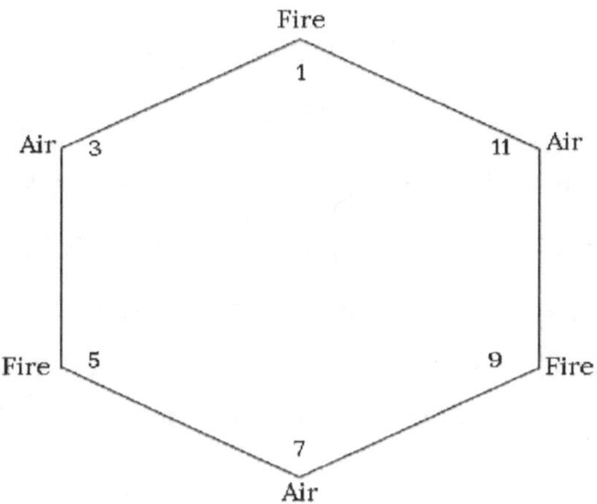

Fire and air support each other. If the element is not helpful then the malefic planet does not give inauspicious results. For example, a bad person hesitates to do wrong activities if the environment and surroundings do not support him.

It is the environment and surroundings that decide what kind of activities a person will do. Similarly, the element of the zodiac sign decides what kind of results the planet will produce.

For example, in Chart 1, suppose a planet is in Aries, then their sextile aspect falls on Gemini. The two elements - fire and air support each other, so, the planets in Aries provide support to the third house. Similarly, if a planet is in the second house in Taurus, then their sextile aspect falls on the 4th house, which is Cancer, earth and water support each other.

3.3 Square

In geometry, a square is formed with four angles that are equal to 90° and has four equal sides. Similarly, when two or more planets are situated at a distance of 90° from each other, they form square aspects. Square is considered a hard (tough) aspect as it creates tension, conflict, and obstacles in life.

But why the square aspect is considered to be a hard aspect?

Because the elements forming such aspects do not support each other. The elements located at a distance of 90° are completely different and their properties are opposite to each other. However, the quality of both the element is same but it doesn't make any difference.

For example, in the above chart, a planet in Aries forms a square aspect with Cancer. The element of Aries is Fire and the element of Cancer is Water, they are completely opposite to each other. Similarly, the planet placed in Taurus forms a square aspect with Leo. The element of Taurus is earth and the element of Leo is fire, they are also opposite to each other. If there is a fire, put water or soil in the fire, the fire will be extinguished.

Therefore, when planets create 90° aspect with each other, the flow of energy blocks which creates various types of tension and struggle in life. We can understand this with the help of the following chart. Suppose, a person is going from west to east and another person is going from south to north. They create blockage for each other when both they meet at the crossroads at the same time and no one is ready to give space to the other. Even though the quality of the person is the same but it doesn't provide any support, and the movement of both of them stops. For example, let's say two people are very good at behavior but they can block each other's path.

Chart 3.1:

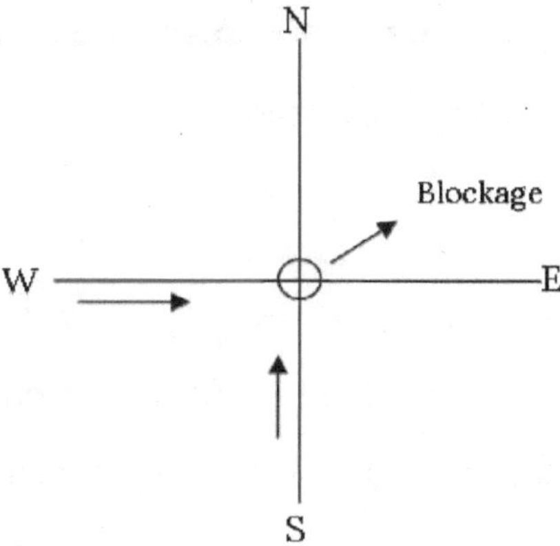

Chart 3.2:

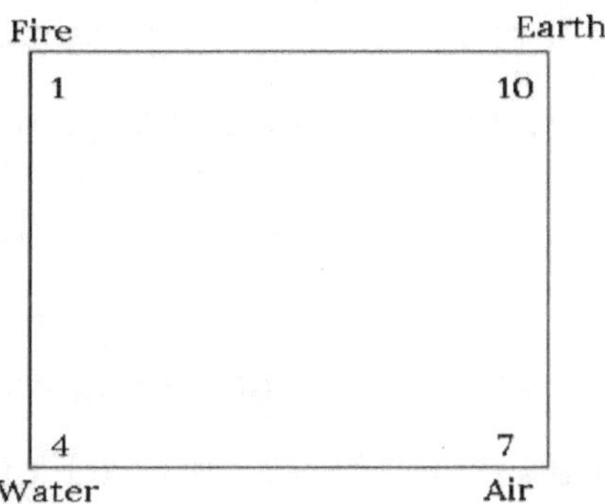

In the same manner, when planets start forming square aspects, then the momentum in life slows down. Gradually, the flow of energy gets blocked in the respective house. Such blockage stops the pace of life and creates various kinds of problems and conflict. When effect of such aspect starts, I observed that, once a work which is going on a good condition suddenly stops, as if someone has poured water on the fire.

When many planets together form a square aspect, it makes the life difficult for the native. A person can fight when a hard aspect comes and goes by one or two planets, but when such aspect simultaneously formed by many planets then such a crisis is called midlife crisis.

However, the positive side of this aspect is that it makes the person stronger in life. Such a person is not easily discouraged and finds his own way forward. When the time is not favourable, they learn how to compromise with the situation. When storm strikes, those trees and grasses that are resilient survive but those that remain upright break through their roots. Time teaches us to be flexible in life when the tide turns against us.

3.4 Trine

When two or more planets are four signs apart or form an angle of 120°, they create a trine aspect with each other. Trine aspect is considered a highly auspicious and favorable aspect. After the difference of 120° in the zodiac, the element of the sign is the same. You can see in the below chart that Aries, Leo, and Sagittarius (1-5-9) form a triangle and all three have fire signs, similarly to others.

Chart4:

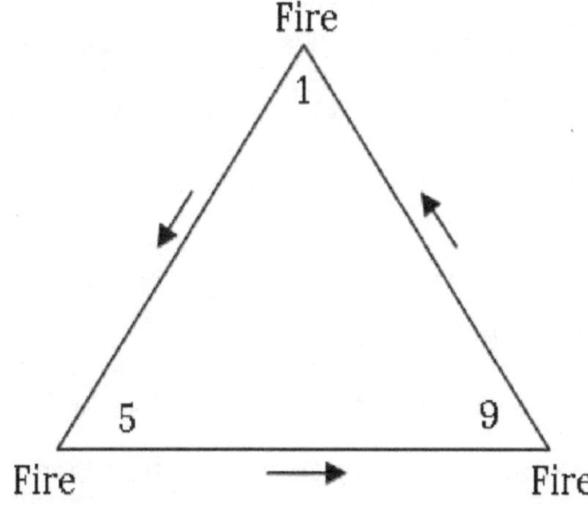

In this aspect, the flow of energy is natural and there is great harmony among the planets situated here. Even the planets who has enmity with each other do not give malefic results and tend to produce their positive results only.

When planets form such aspects, the tailwinds start in the life of the person. Opportunity knocks at the door and everything goes very smoothly in life. Because everything goes well, one gets success very easily. However, the negative side of such an aspect is that it makes the person lazy, haughty, and arrogant. When the going gets easy the enthusiasm to fight the tide wanes and one soon becomes disheartened in difficult situations.

3.5 Opposition

When two or more planets are exactly 180° apart from each other, they create an opposition aspect. Such a difference in the orb is the 7th sign in the zodiac from where the planet is currently posited. The 7th element in the zodiac is a complementary element like; Fire (1) – Air (7), Earth (2) – Water (8), Air (3) – Fire (9), Water (4) – Earth (10) and represents the same quality, like; Movable – Movable, Fixed – Fixed, Dual - Dual.

In the above Chart 1, you can see that Aries is the first sign which is a Fire and Movable sign and from here 180° apart is the 7th sign Libra which is an Air and Movable sign. The element in these two signs are complementary to each other, Fire – Air, and both have the same Movable quality.

The energy generated by a planet in Aries is different from the same planet produced in Libra, as the element is different. Hence, such an aspect creates pressure, tension, and conflict in life as there is a lack of harmony between these two energies. For example, Saturn which is a dry and cold planet in the fire sign (Aries) produces a different kind of energy in the natal chart, and Saturn in the Air sign (Libra) produces a different kind of energy in transit and there is no harmony between these two energies. Although the element supports each other but planetary energy is different. Due to such disharmony when a planet in the natal chart creates opposition with the same planet in transit, various tensions and conflicts start to arise in the life of the natives related to the matter of the concerned houses.

In the same manner, a planet in Taurus which is Earth and a Fixed sign creates opposition to Scorpio which is Water and a Fixed sign and so on.

Due to disharmony of energies although the opposition aspect creates stress, pressure, the difference of opinion, and conflict in life, but element supports each other, so support also come. Also, both the signs have the same quality, therefore, deep inside they feel attraction toward each other; Movable (1) - Movable (7), Fixed (2) – Fixed (8), Dual (3) – Dual (9).

This is why it is said that opposites attract. Each house from the seventh house represents not only tension and conflict but also attraction and support. The first house in the zodiac represents yourself and the seventh house represents your spouse or partner. Lovers attract and support each other but stress, tension, and difference of opinion are also a part of life from which one cannot escape. It is the functioning of the opposite aspect (7th house) which will accompany you, due to which you will feel the attraction but will also give stress and tension in life.

Chart 5:

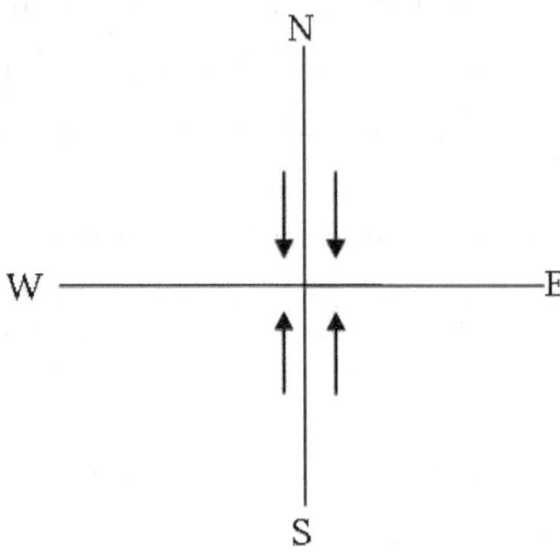

The above chart represents the energy coming from two different directions. Such a situation in life teaches us to create balance in every sphere of life. The opposition represents the polarities and without balance, it cannot exist. It is the meeting of two opposite energies like yin and yang. When two opposite energies of similar quality meet it provides an opportunity for a union. It also indicates a compromise without which a union of two different energy is not possible and then such a situation becomes a stalemate in life. The crisis of middle age teaches a person to make compromises in various aspects of life.

3.6 Planetary Aspects - Vedic Astrology

According to Hindu astrology, a planet cannot aspect any other planet or bhava with 30° in front of it and 60° behind it. The aspect starts at 30° in front of a planet and it stops at 300° from the planet.

All Planets aspect 7th house from the position occupied by them. However, Mars, Jupiter, Saturn, and Rahu have special aspects besides the 7th aspect. The planetary aspects are as under:

• Sun, Mercury, Venus - 7th aspect

• Mars – 4th, 7th and 8th aspect

• Jupiter and Rahu- 5th, 7th and 9th aspect

• Saturn - 3rd, 7th and 10th aspect

Note:

• Sextile is similar to 3rd aspect

• Square is similar to 4th aspect

• Trine is similar to 5th aspect

• Opposition is similar to 7th aspect

Chapter 4

The Planets

Vedic astrology considers the influence of nine planets in our birth chart. Sun, Moon, Mercury, Venus, Mars, Jupiter, Saturn, and two shadow planets Rahu and Ketu. Each planet represents its own unique characteristics, which affect the physical and mental activities of the individual and the things around him.

The Sun and the Moon are the two luminaries in the sky that are not planets, the other five being planets and can be seen from the Earth. Rahu and Ketu being shadow planets are not visible, but the subtle energy of these two planets affects the life of the person and the conditions of the earth. All Planets aspect 7th house from the position occupied by them. However, Mars, Jupiter, Saturn, and Rahu have special aspects besides the 7th aspect. Ketu has no aspect.

Planets and their Characteristics

4.1 The Sun

The Sun is considered to be the king of universe. It is a symbol of the soul and the 'Lord of Sunday'. The Sun moves in only one direction, never retrogrades, stay one month in a sign, and completes the entire zodiac in a year. It is the center of the solar system and everything revolves around the Sun.

In India, we worship Surya as the Sun God, who is the supreme giver and everything on this earth originated from the Sun. The Sun is life, without the Sun there is no life on earth. Sun is exalted at 10 degrees in Aries and powerful in the other two fire signs; Leo and Sagittarius. It is debilitated at 10 degrees in Libra and faces difficulties in the other two air signs; Gemini and Aquarius. Its own sign and Mooltrikona sign both is Leo.

Astronomy: The Sun is the centre of the solar system. It is the biggest object and contains 99.8% of the solar system's mass. It is about 150 million kilometres from Earth. Its gravity holds the solar system together. It is not a solid mass; it is composed of layers made up almost entirely of hydrogen and helium. The surface of the Sun is about 10,000 degrees Fahrenheit (5,500 degrees Celsius) hot, while temperatures in the core reach more than 27 million F (15 million C). It has a well-known sunspot cycle which has a maximum of around every 11 years. The Sun is the source of enormous amount of energy, part of which provides the light and heat needed to support life on Earth.

Direction and Digbala: The direction of the Sun is east. It gets directional strength (Digbala) in the 10th house and weakness when it is placed in the 4th house.

Classification: It is the Sattvic planet and controls our consciousness. It is a fiery, dry, and masculine planet. Its colour is red and the caste is Kshatriya. It controls metals - gold, copper, and ruby. It represents coarse clothes and the age of 50 years old. It represents the summer season and organic matter. It represents bones, average height, steadfast tendency, and upward direction. It represents places of worship and temples, mountain trees, and pungent taste like; onion, ginger, black pepper, chilies, etc.

Characteristics: The Sun is 'Self' and 'Esteem'. It provides illumination and warmth. The shining Sun in the sky represents strength, energy, and vitality. It represents the power of resistance. It is bold and forceful. It represents mental strength and confidence. It is ego and pride. It represents father, authority, government, honor from government, high status, fame, victory, and enlightenment. Strong Sun in the horoscope makes a person determined and decisive. It gives high energy, commanding power, quality of leadership, respect of elders, and good quality of listening.

A strong Sun represents a charismatic personality. The person will be ambitious, energetic, influential, and kind-hearted. The person will be courageous enough to go alone, even in difficult circumstances without any fear. He will not be ready to compromise anything for his dignity and honor. In my corporate career, I have seen that people are ready to quit their jobs but are not ready to compromise on their dignity if the Sun is strong on their chart. They are ready to bear anything in life for their self-respect. In such a situation, worshiping the Sun God daily is beneficial for the person.

Sun gets exalted in Aries, a fiery sign of Mars. Aries represents the solo spirit and does not wait for others to come. Aries means – at the top of the mountain alone. The nature of this sign is suitable for the Sun – King, so, it is exalted here. While Libra is a marketplace, is totally against the tendency of the Sun. Therefore, the Sun gets debilitated in Libra.

Sun controls our eyesight, to regain eye-sight and vitality in life people in India worship Lord Sun. When the sunlight comes everything is visible. In the same way, wherever the Sun is placed in your chart everything will become visible and you cannot hide it.

Affliction: If Sun is afflicted in a chart, then the person will easily become tempered, arrogant, jealous, irritable, dominating, pretentious, lavish, conceit, and haughty. Such people do not listen to anyone's advice and consider themselves supreme. They are not ready to change their ideas/plans under any circumstances and expect others to accept them.

Body parts and diseases: Sun rules our head, brain, eyes, heart, lungs, blood, and circulation. Diseases; blood pressure, eye diseases, fever, cerebral disorders, etc.

4.2 The Moon

The Moon is the earth's only natural satellite. It is considered the queen of the solar system. It moves 13.2 degrees per day, completes one orbit around the earth in 27.3 days, and rises on an average 50 minutes late every day. The half of the Moon which is towards the Sun can be seen from the earth and is called the phases of the Moon.

The cycle of lunar phases takes 29.5 days, known as the synodic period, which is longer than the sidereal period of 27.3 days. The reason for this difference is the Moon returns to the same place in the sky once every sidereal period, but the Sun is also moving in the sky. When the Moon returns to the same place in the sky, the Sun moves 27 degrees. It takes the Moon about two days to catch this difference. Moon's own sign is Cancer, it gets exalted in Taurus at 3 degrees which is also its Mooltrikona sign, it gets debilitated in Scorpio at 3 degrees.

Understanding the different phases of the Moon is very important in astrology. When the Moon is exactly opposite the Sun (180° or 7th house) in a horoscope, it is a full moon day. Moon is considered weak within 72 degrees from the Sun. Amavasya (new moon) occurs when Sun and Moon both are in the same house and less than 13.2 degrees from each other.

Astronomy: The Moon is the only natural satellite of the Earth. Its average distance from Earth is 385,000 km and the Earth rotates on its axis once every 27.3 days (a sidereal month). Its daytime temperature is 225°F (107°C), while night-time temperatures are -243°F (-153°C). It has a solid, rocky surface covered with craters, mountain ranges, rills (long narrow channels), and lava plains.

Direction and Digbala: The direction of the Moon is North-West; it gets directional strength (Digbala) in the 4th house and weakness in the 10th house.

Classification: Moon is a watery planet, represents moist and rainy season and watery places like; well, water tanks, bathrooms, watery surfaces, rivers, bays, ocean, etc. Its color is white and indicates a small height. It represents new fabric and organic matter. It represents salty taste (sea salt, rock salt), gems, spotless pearls, silver, and other white metals. It belongs to the Vaishya caste and represents the age of 70 years old. It represents the coconut tree, fruits, vegetables, and all watery substances.

Characteristics: Moon is a Sattvik planet and controls our minds. It is a feminine planet, represents mother in the chart, peace of mind, and rules our emotions. It represents selflessness like a mother and the tender qualities of a female. It represents the nourishing quality, sensitivity, and imagination of the person. A strong Moon indicates a strong mind, friendly nature, and pleasing personality. The person is receptive, decisive, mature, helpful in nature, and clear in his thoughts. Such a person never wastes time in vain things, wants the discussion to come to the point, and takes no interest in idle gossip.

Being the representative of the mother in the horoscope, the person should always respect his mother and should never quarrel with her, if the person wants that his Moon always remains strong.

Moon rules over the masses, the 4th house is the house of the masses, if Moon is situated in the 4th house, then the popularity of the person is indicated. Moon being a feminine planet bestows attractiveness and other feminine qualities. The person under the influence of the Moon as a ruling planet takes interest in taking care of others. It indicates professions related to fluids, doctors, psychologists, therapists, child care, and other nurturing and healing professions.

The Sun represents the father, the moon represents the mother; The Sun represents the seed, the Moon represents the womb; The Sun represents the order and the Moon represents the fulfillment of the order. The Moon has no light and is always dependent on sunlight; The Sun shows independence and the weak Moon indicates that the person is looking for support and is always afraid of being alone. The Sun represents the present, the Moon represents the past. If Moon is situated in any house from the 9th to 12th house, then the person takes interest in subjects like; History, Archaeology, Astrology, etc. The person memorizes the dates of historical events easily and is quick to learn these subjects.

When the Moon placed less than 72 degrees from the Sun, it indicates less sunlight and due to absence of sunlight the native is prone to diseases easily. Such native must worship lord Sun in his whole life.

The sign of Taurus is highly suitable for the Moon. Taurus is a feminine sign – fertile and receptive, it is a highly fertile land in the zodiac. The nature of Taurus is to produce and grow things.

Its symbol is the bull which is known for its sensuality and fertility. Taurus represents luxury and comfort, therefore, the Moon – the Queen, finds this sign perfectly suitable for herself, and becomes exalted at 3 degrees in the sign (Upon entering here, the queen found a very suitable place for her stay). Scorpio is a sign of ruthlessness and represents muddy water which is totally against the nature of the Moon – the Queen, and it gets debilitated in the sign while entering (3 degrees).

Affliction: An afflicted moon indicates a person will become depressed, pessimistic, impulsive, timid and over-anxious, dreamers, self-destructive, insane, and psychic. A weak moon indicates a person can be easily influenced by outside energies and unable to take decisive decisions.

Body parts and diseases: The organs ruled by the Moon are; Blood, saliva, womb, abdomen, and breasts of women. According to medical astrology, surgical operations should be avoided during the full moon as there is more fluid at this time. Diseases; cough and cold, lunacy, paralysis, hysteria, epilepsy, etc.

4.3 Mars

The Red Planet Mars is considered the Commander-in-Chief of the Solar System and denotes strength in the horoscope. According to Hindu mythology, Mars is called Mangal or Bhauma and is believed to be the brother (or son) of Earth. Mars represents energy, either constructive or destructive. It shows our ambition, passion, and desire. Energy should always be controlled as it can lead us to act indiscriminately without thinking or with no direction, and it can create problems. Mars becomes exalted at 28° in Capricorn and debilitated at 28° in Cancer. It rules over Aries and Scorpio, where first it has a positive sign and later it has a negative sign.

Astronomy: Mars, the fourth planet from the Sun, is easily seen in the sky - a bright red dot in the sky. Mars is easiest to observe when it and the Sun are on opposite sides in the sky. Its distance from the Sun is 228 million km. Mars orbits the Sun once in 687 Earth days and completes one revolution every 24.6 hours. Mars has a thin atmosphere composed of carbon dioxide, nitrogen, and argon, its surface is covered by loose dust and rock. Its soil is rich in iron gives its red colour. It has about one-tenth the mass of Earth. Mars has two moons, Phobos and Deimos.

Direction and Digbala: The direction of Mars is South; it gets directional strength (Digbala) in the 10th house and weakness in the 4th house.

Classification: Mars is considered a Tamasic and fiery planet. It is a masculine and Kshatriya caste planet. It is a dry and barren planet and indicates a tense and quarrelsome situation. It represents accidents, fires, disputes, destruction, wars, and sexual drive. Its colour is blood-red and stone coral. It represents the summer season and fiery places. It deals with burnt clothing and inorganic substances. It represents young age and low height. Its metal is iron, the taste is bitter and the tendency is violent. It represents upward movement.

Characteristics: Mars is considered a malefic and ruthless planet. Being the lord of weapons and war, Mars does not think twice. If it is favorable in the horoscope, it bestows good qualities; One will be courageous, will fight evils, and will do heroic deeds. The character of a person is strong, determined, passionate and the person is not afraid of any kind of obstacles in life. He is a great protector and always uses his sword to protect others. He can go to any extent to save someone's life.

Mars represents the drive, courage, initiation, and adventurous nature of the person. It represents determination, confidence, sharp wit, and leadership quality. The position of Mars in the birth chart shows where the physical activity will take place and indicates what kind of things will excite you, how you deal with disputes and react to stressful situations, violence, etc. Mars represents the younger brother, land, and property and rules the animal instincts in man. Mars believes in overcoming obstacles by force rather than any strategy. This indicates the impulsive nature of a person with a quick activity.

Martians are the pioneers and have risk-taking inclinations. It belongs to entrepreneurs, conquerors, adventurers, and athletes. They like to conduct large-scale operations that requires high energy. Mars indicates new ventures and its beneficial aspects indicate the floating of new companies.

As Commander-in-Chief, the most important thing for Mars is to win the battle. Similarly, the most important thing for a quarrelsome person is to win the argument, no matter how. Therefore, a wise man never indulges in any discussion with such a person. An afflicted Mars indicates that the person can go to any extreme to win the argument and fight.

Mars represents action and energy. Action without a goal is a waste of energy. The energy of Mars should be used in a constructive manner and in spiritual activities. Mars gets exalted in Capricorn, a sign of Saturn. Capricorn represents a high level of restrictions and control. In this sign, Martian energy is fully controlled, when energy is fully controlled it produces maximum results. Mars gets exalted at 28 degrees in Capricorn, at this point, Mars energy is fully controlled (however, Saturn treats Mars as its enemy). Cancer, a sign of the Moon has no power to control Martian energy. Therefore, Mars gets debilitated in this sign.

We move into this world due to Martian energy. To burn energy, fuel is required and that fuel is our desire. If the fuel (desire) produces smoke, it not only disturbs the life of the person but also the environment around him. Mars represents fire, and the scar of fire does not go easily. Therefore, one must control Martian energy in a constructive manner so that it should not produce smoke and should not leave a scar.

Mars indicates physical sports and exercise, the iron and steel industry, police department, firefighting department, military activities, etc. It represents fiery places like; the kitchen, engine room, and boilers. It indicates cuts, wounds, scars, strikes, conspiracy, criminals, murderers, thieves, robbers, etc.

Affliction: If the planet is afflicted then the person will use all his power to fulfil his desire and can go to any extent. Irrespective of how many fingers are burnt, the fulfilment of desire is very important for him and if the person is running on the Mahadasha of Mars, then dangerous consequences can be possible, as he is not ready to give up his desire under any circumstances. A weak and afflicted Mars makes the native a sexual pervert.

The afflicted Mars indicates that the native will easily lose his temper and start abusing others without thinking. The person will become quarrelsome and will be ready to fight over trivial matters; Scratches on a car and people are ready to fight on the street. The afflicted Mars does not like differences of opinion with anyone. The native will argue in vain, instead of giving any intelligent argument, he prefers to use force and feels the joy of winning the battle.

Body Parts and diseases: Bone marrow, forehead, nose, urinary system, external sex organs, prostate gland, muscle tissue, etc. Diseases: Bleeding, menstrual disorders, abortion, smallpox, chickenpox, fistula, burns, cuts, wounds, measles, malaria, diseases of the bone marrow, etc.

4.4 Mercury

Mercury is considered as Prince of the solar system and "Messenger to the Gods". As per Hindu mythology, Mercury is a child of the Moon. Mercury rules our intelligence, intellect, memory, reasoning, power of speech, etc. It is a planet of trade and commerce and represents all financial activities. Mercury gets exalted at 15° in Virgo and debilitated at 15° in Pisces. It rules over Gemini and Virgo, where first it has a positive sign and later it has a negative sign.

Astronomy: Mercury is the smallest planet in the solar system and nearest to the Sun. It does not go beyond 28° from the Sun. Mercury is only 1.4 times larger than Moon and it is only visible in the sky at the time of sunrise and sunset. It takes 88 Earth days to complete a single orbit around the Sun. Because the planet is so close to the Sun, its surface temperatures are both extremely hot and cold. The day temperatures can reach highs of 430°C and at night temperatures can dip as low as -180°C. Mercury is not the hottest planet, it is Venus because of its dense atmosphere.

Direction and Digbala: The direction of Mercury is North; it gets directional strength (Digbala) in the 1st house and weakness in the 7th house.

Classification: Mercury is a rajasic planet, its colour is green, and the stone is emerald. It is considered a boy and represents playgrounds and living beings. Its metal is alloy and the gender is a eunuch. It belongs to the Vaishya caste and represents wet clothes. It represents mixed tastes and a mixture of diverse qualities. It represents skin, short in height, and sideways momentum. It represents wet crop, brinjal, ladyfinger, beetroot, etc. It belongs to the Sharad season (from 20 Sept. to 19 Nov. approx.).

Characteristics: Mercury is considered to be a child and children tend to imitate elders, similarly, Mercury reflects the characteristics of the planet with which it is associated. Children must be nurtured by their parents and elders. Similarly, Mercury must be associated with benefics. Mercury alone in a house or its association with malefics does not produce good results.

Mercury indicates how we express ourselves to the outside world. It indicates literary pursuit and makes a person good at speaking, learning, proficient in many languages, and orator. It represents analytical ability, planning, diplomacy, accounting, ideas, thoughts, talkative person, jokes, intelligence, writing, editing, publishing, etc. It indicates universities, colleges, schools, shops, and market place.

Mercury creates a sharp mind, awareness, deep research, and mystery seekers. Strong mercury is required to be good at maths and astrology. It indicates that the person will be able to grasp the subject quickly, have good retentive power, and will be strong in mental calculations. Mercury indicates connections, many friends, correspondence, news, and information. Mercury is mutable and represents restlessness nature and lack of consistency. Therefore, Mercurians must learn stability and perseverance in their lives. The placement of mercury in a chart indicates an inquisitive and curious person. It shows the dexterity, ingenuity, and versatile nature of the person. However, if the person possesses a firm and steady attitude and leaves his restless nature then he will perform better in his work. Because Mercury's nature is mutable, it indicates that if a person involves themselves in overindulgence in a work, then he will leave it after some time.

Mercury's exaltation sign is Virgo – a Mooltrikona sign of Mercury. The sign of Virgo represents virginity and celibacy. Mercury is considered an adolescent as it is yet to attain maturity. Mercury exalted in Virgo indicates that a teenager should follow the path of celibacy to make his mind sharp. Pisces represents sexual pleasure, if a teenager indulges in sexual activities, his Mercury will be debilitated and he will lose courage and ability to speak when needed. Indulgence in sexual activity will also hamper the development of his mind. Such a person will not get a sharp mind in his life, he will remain a person of a very mediocre mind and will never be able to become an intelligent and wise person.

Mercury represents mixed flavour; hence, Mercurians find pleasure in variety. Poor mercury indicates lack of concentration, changing moods, and poor memory. Mercury in the 6th house indicates that the native may have a problem with forgetting. Mercury in the 4th house indicates the person will have to live in many houses.

Affliction: Mercury is the lord of green colour, if it is afflicted then gradually the green colour will disappear from the native's life. Afflicted mercury indicates native will be cunning, liar, eccentric, scandalous, cheater, argumentative, unprincipled, and boastful. It shows the person may be gullible or will cheat his clients and run away with their money.

Body Parts and diseases: Mercury represents the brain, vein, skin, tongue, nervous system, thyroid gland, neck, etc. Diseases: loss of memory, skin diseases, dumbness, stammering, nervous system disorder, whimsical, giddiness, impotency, insomnia, etc.

4.5 Jupiter

Jupiter is known as the Prime minister in the planetary cabinet and is considered as Dev Guru. It is a fruitful and a "Highly Benefic" planet in astrology. It represents optimism, aspiration, knowledge, and wisdom. The planet of abundance is noble and benevolent. It provides dignity, reputation, and expansion. It rules over finance and family and represents an honest and sincere person. It represents administration and economic activity and rules over law and religion. It is called "The planet of Fortune". Jupiter gets exalted at 5° in Cancer and debilitated at 5° in Capricorn. It rules over Sagittarius and Pisces, where first it has a positive sign and later it has a negative sign.

Astronomy: Jupiter is the largest planet in the solar system, it is more than twice as massive as all the other planets combined. Jupiter's immense volume could hold more than 1,300 Earths. Jupiter has 79 known moons, one year on Jupiter is the same as

11.8 Earth years. Jupiter is a gas giant and doesn't have a solid surface. It has big storms like the Great Red Spot, that's about twice the size of Earth and has raged for over a century.

Direction and Digbala: The direction of Jupiter is North-East; it gets directional strength (Digbala) in the 1st house and weakness in the 7th house.

Classification: Jupiter is considered a watery and sattvic planet. It is a masculine, brahmin caste planet and represents ether. It indicates treasury, storeroom, and places where money and jewels are deposited. Its colour is yellow, the stone is yellow sapphire, topaz and metal is gold. It represents a gentle tendency and sweet taste. It represents fat constituents and tall height. It deals with medium clothes, living beings, and age of 30 years old. It indicates Hemant season (20th Nov. to 19th Jan. approx.) and evenly momentum.

Characteristics: Jupiter is considered to be 'The Master'. It represents the generosity of the person. Being Dev Guru, one should always respect Jupiter. In the same manner, the person having strong Jupiter attracts respect from others. Jupiter is considered a consular and represents all counselling activities. Jupiter provides wisdom and removes ignorance and darkness. A strong Jupiter indicates a very honest person. He is dutiful and respects law and religion. He is a magnanimous and broad-minded person and does not believe in any type of fighting and works on making the atmosphere congenial. He believes in co-operation, works on a strategy, and waits for the outcome patiently.

Jupiter provides education, interest in religion, spiritual rhymes, philosophy, astrology, and law. A strong Jupiter indicates concentration, mediation, reading habits, thrust for knowledge, benevolence, prudent behaviour, ethics, morals, etc. Jupiter represents abundance, when it is favourable, opportunity knocks on your door. A person having strong Jupiter in his chart never breaches anyone's trust. The person will always show respect to others, favour doing the right things, and follow the path of justice.

Jupiter always prevents the native from difficulties till the native follow the righteous path in his life. The person will be protected at the last moment in a state of difficulty when every possible hope is over. Like a guru teaches lessons to his students and provides his guidance and protection as long as the student follows the guru's advice, but when the student stops listening to the guru after several warnings, the guru simply removes his protective shield. This is the way Jupiter works.

Jupiter punishes the person but not like Mars. Mars's attack is direct and sharp but Jupiter simply goes away without saying anything. Without the absence of Jupiter gradually the guidance of direction removes from the person's life and his worthless wandering starts with no outcome. The darkness of ignorance submerges the person. When Jupiter becomes malefic, he removes his shield and stops giving direction. Without direction, the person wanders here and there and wastes his time and energy.

Jupiter represents growth, and the freshwater of Cancer represents life as well as growth. Therefore, Jupiter feels most comfortable in the sign of Cancer and gets exalted here. Cancer is the fourth sign of the zodiac which is ruled by the Moon. The fourth house also represents the mother's womb. A pregnant woman is the best example of Jupiter exalted in Cancer. The unborn baby (fetus) growing in the womb floats in the fluid, life is expanding in the water.

Swami Vivekananda said, "Strength is Life, Weakness is Death. Expansion is Life, Contraction is Death. Love is Life, Hatred is Death". Jupiter represents all the positive qualities said in the quote.

Jupiter represents a person who fulfils his promises and never breaches anyone's trust if a person does against this then Jupiter removes its shield of protection. Jupiter gets debilitated in Capricorn; a sign ruled by Saturn. Capricorn is a sign of a high level of control, restrictions, and limitations. A planet of expansion – Jupiter, feels completely hapless in this sign. A debilitated Jupiter in a chart indicates that a person wants to do various things in his life, but has to face a problem of lack of resources. He will complete the task only by moving inch by inch.

Jupiter rules our big plans and bestows us, children. When a couple has a child, various necessities of the child start and they take interest in the fulfilment of all these activities, representing the expansion of life in this mundane world. Children are our future; therefore, Jupiter represents the future.

Jupiter is also our luck; therefore, people say when someone is going to do an act when the outcome is unknown "Best of Luck", seeking the blessings of Lord Jupiter. Jupiter represents the person who follows principles and does not deviate from the chosen path. Materialistic desire does not allure the person, he prefers to face any situation in life but does not ready to surrender his respect.

Jupiter represents; schools and colleges, law-court, temples, places of sermons, legislative assembly, charitable institutions, bank buildings, hospitals, asylums, and all fatty and sweet products. Jupiter represents the husband in the female horoscope. If a native is running from Jupiter Mahadasha or in transit affected by Jupiter, the native has the inclination to eat more sweets than his normal eating.

Physicians write "Rx" at the top of the prescription before writing their medical advice and seek the blessings of Jupiter. Rx is the Latin symbol for the planet Jupiter. Medical astrology states that taking medicine in Jupiter Hora is more beneficial than at any other time.

In which house Jupiter is situated represents an expansion on matters related to the house. Jupiter's placement in a chart indicates a person will adopt ethical principles and take interest in the expansion of activities related to the house concerned. It also indicates our luck resides there.

Affliction: An afflicted Jupiter makes the person extremists and fanatics. It will put the person into the ocean of darkness and due to lack of knowledge the person will not listen to anyone. Due to his boastful nature, he will wander here and there with no fruitful outcome. Afflicted Jupiter indicates false optimism, false faith, and orthodox beliefs. A weak Jupiter indicates, a lack of hope, absence of knowledge, greed, materialistic nature, extravagant, overconfident, lazy, worthless promises, etc. The native will not be a liberal person, instead of dutiful he will be careless. Show false reputation to others. Shy away from religious activities, chanting spiritual rhymes is very difficult for him. He will always do improper judgments and make mistakes in calculations.

Body Parts and diseases: Jupiter represents the liver, circulation of blood in the arteries, pancreas, hips, thighs fat in the body. Diseases: Problem in liver, flatulence, jaundice, diabetes, eczema, hernia, etc.

4.6 Venus

Venus is considered a Demon Guru. According to Hindu mythology, the demon Guru has only one eye. Venus is said to be Mahalakshmi, the wife of Lord Vishnu. It is considered the goddess of love. It bestows marriage, beauty, and grace to the person. It offers luxury and comfort. Venus is exalted at 27° in Pisces and debilitated at 27° in Virgo. It rules over Taurus and Libra, where first it has a negative sign and later it has a positive sign.

Astronomy: Venus is the hottest planet in the Solar System and is much closer to the Sun than Earth. It has a dense atmosphere filled with clouds composed of the greenhouse gas carbon dioxide and sulfuric acid. The gas traps heat and keeps Venus warm. Earth is just a little bit bigger than the size of Venus. Venus is unusual because it spins on its axis from east to west i.e., it moves in the opposite direction of Earth and most other planets. It takes about 243 Earth days to spin around just once. It does not go beyond 48° from the Sun. Venus sets after Sunset and rises before the Sun rises. Venus orbits the Sun once every seven and a half months (224.7 days). On Venus, the Sun rises every 117 Earth days, which means the Sun rises two times each year on Venus. Venus is an evening star for about nine months until it passes behind the Sun, then a morning star for nine months as it moves between the Sun and Earth.

Direction and Digbala: The direction of Venus is South-East; it gets directional strength (Digbala) in the 4th house.

Classification: Venus is considered a warm and rajasic planet. It is a feminine, brahmin caste planet and represents fresh water. Its colour is variegated and represents diamonds and pearls. It represents excellent cloth and bedrooms. Its taste is sour and the tendency is light. It rules over all exotic vegetables, potatoes, cabbages, fruit trees, flower trees, creeping plants, and organic matter. It represents the average height and age of 16 years old. It indicates Vasant season and sideways momentum.

Characteristics: Venus represents a charming personality. Venusians are kind and friendly. It rules over marriage and represents the wife in the male horoscope. It rules over all kinds of beauty, pleasures, and luxuries of life. It makes a person generous and cheerful. It provides peace in the relationship. Venus must be strong in a chart to make a good career in art and music, it gives a melodious and pleasing voice to the person.

Being a feminine planet Venus presents feminine qualities, they are gentle and show graceful manners, they avoid quarrels and turmoil at any cost, and try to lead a happy and peaceful life. They are soft-spoken and rarely show their anger on their face, when they are angry, they try to remain silent. They are caring in nature and take care of each member of the family. They are the person who works as a bridge in the family. The house in which Venus is situated in the horoscope of the native, the person always likes cleanliness in matters related to that house. For example, if Venus is in the Ascendant, then the person will take care of his clothes and like to eat quality food, such a person never accepts anything degraded.

Venus represents feminine energy and love. Love demands attention. The relationship will dry and come to an end if you do not properly feed the relationship. In the same way, in which house Venus has placed, the activities related to the house require your attention. A favorable Venus indicates a good relationship with partners, easy negotiations, and a win-win situation.

Venus is exalted in the twelfth house and it is the house of salvation. Venus rules the semen and sexual energy of the human body. The rotation of Venus in the opposite direction of Earth indicates the transformation of sexual energy into spiritual energy, it shows that when the sexual energy moves against the gravitational force of Earth i.e., upward, and reaches the Sahasrara Chakra (Crown Chakra), one will become enlightened. This is the reason why Venus is exalted in the house of Jupiter (the 12th house is the house of Jupiter and Jupiter considers Venus as its enemy). The debilitation of Venus in the 6th house indicates a wastage of sexual energy.

Venus represents; Cinema Hall, dancing room, bedroom, banquet, textiles, automobiles, cars, ships, airplanes, glass industry, confectionery, perfume, embroidery, milk, paint, sandal, soar fruits, jewellery, dress, vehicle, sexual pleasure, flowers, drinking water, hotels, honour, respect, female boss, business relation with females, catering, toys, delicious food, juice, drinks, etc.

Affliction: An afflicted Venus indicates over-Indulgence in sexual activities, loss of a partner, separation from the beloved, excessive marriages, loss of prestige, scandals, always looking for some amusement, fond of fancy food and overeating, drinking, company of bad friends, etc. An afflicted Venus denies the marriage, it indicates quarrels with the partner or a breakup in the relationship. The person will lead an immoral life, obsessed with desires, jealous, and vengeful. Accidents through animals and birds are also indicated by afflicted Venus.

Body Parts and diseases: Eyes, Reproductive organ, Semen, Kidney. Diseases: Problem in eyes, Ovaries, Hysteria, Eczema, Leprosy, Leukoderma, etc.

4.7 Saturn

As per Hindu astrology, Saturn is the son of the Sun. It is called "Yama" and chief governor for longevity and death. Saturn gets exalted at 20° in Libra and debilitated at 20° in Aries. It rules over Capricorn and Aquarius, where first it has a negative sign and later it has a positive sign.

Astronomy: Saturn is the sixth planet from the Sun and the second-largest planet in our solar system. It is a gas giant composed mainly of gases and liquid. It has beautiful rings which are made of pieces of ice, dust, and rock. It is the farthest planet from Earth that is visible to the naked human eye. Saturn completes one revolution of the Sun in 29.5 Earth years.

Direction and Digbala: The direction of Saturn is West; it gets directional strength (Digbala) in the 7th house and weakness in the 1st house.

Classification: Saturn is an airy, dry, cold, and tamasic planet. It is a shudra caste planet and its gender is neutral. Its colour is blue, the metal is iron and lead, and the stone is sapphire. It represents rags, torn clothes, and inorganic matter. It governs the muscles, indicates a tall person, and is related to old age. Its taste is astringent and the tendency is hard. It belongs to thorny and poisonous trees, broom, bitter gourd, onion, drumstick, betel leaves, tobacco, and greens. Its season is Sisira (January-March) and the momentum is downward.

Characteristics: Saturn is a very powerful planet and its effect on life is subtle and more than any other planet, but its effect is very slow and not easily visible. Only those who have the quality of patience can see the effect of Saturn. It controls our muscles, hair, and nails. Our muscles change, but we don't know when; Our hair and nails grow and we don't know when they grew, this is how the energy of Saturn works - gradually and slowly.

Saturn is an icy cold, windy and dry planet. This indicates that things become cold and dry when Saturn's influence begins. Once very warm relations, become cold; A hot business turns sluggish and things freeze like ice. According to Hindu astrology, Saturn is said to be 'lame' which indicates the slow movement of the planet. Due to the influence of Saturn, various activities start slowing down and things do not move as fast as they were earlier.

The downward movement of Saturn indicates that it will bring down the person to earth and show the real truth of life.

Due to the Saturnine effect the person will always reach late, the journey will be delayed, projects will not complete on time. Airplanes, trains, and buses run late.

A strong Saturn indicates; honesty, reliability, truthfulness, balance in judgment, dutifulness, piousness, meditation, and concentration. Saturn bestows discipline, perseverance, responsibility, patience, endurance, stability, control, and frugality. Under the influence of Saturn, the person will grow a beard and do penance. It brings separation, silence, isolation, disease, old age, death, poverty, ugliness, and destruction.

Saturn is alert and careful; It rules over secret matters. It controls unfair judgment and brings balance. It brings limits and hates haste and works only after due consideration. Saturn is the protector and represents protection and security. A security guard must be tall and courageous. Persons under the influence of Saturn are tall and courageous.

Saturn is the son of the Sun but an enemy. Saturn is stubborn but does justice to everyone. Sun represents father and government. When there is a dispute between father and son or there is a problem with the government, then it is an indication of the relationship between Saturn and the Sun.

When a person is suffering from a period of despair or depression, then he goes into a dark room and reduces all hope, Saturn is darkness and despair. Therefore, to overcome such a situation, a person should not sit in a dark room with the lights off and he must remove all the negative energies around him. Saturn is isolation and filth; Such persons will keep themselves in isolation and avoid cleaning their rooms and clothes. Saturn represents stale and cold foods; The person loses all interest in the food and starts eating stale food. Saturn is slow and lethargic; one loses all interest and becomes very slow in his daily activities. (Readers can refer to my book 'Psychology and Investment' to know more about depression)

People under the influence of Saturn prefer cold than hot. They prefer to eat ice cream than tea or coffee. They like to eat preserved foods, but remember Saturn is very stubborn. Excessive consumption of Saturnine products will make a person very stubborn. In my opinion, this could be one of the reasons why kids nowadays are so stubborn and they don't listen to their parents. Each planet controls certain food items and by eating such a thing, such a planet gets strength.

Saturn creates; obstacles, impediments, hindrances and will make the way difficult for the native. Human nature is that whatever you get for free, you will not appreciate it. Saturn teaches hard lessons to the person so that he gives importance to whatever he has gained or achieved.

Saturn represents fog, mist, and dust. People influenced by Saturn think a lot and cannot decide what to do. A weak Saturn indicates that the person is unable to take the right decision, their mind is clouded and they cannot see a clear picture. In case of any wrong deeds, a weak Saturnian person tries to spread dust on the matter and hide it, so that others also do not see a clear picture.

Saturn is exalted in Libra; Saturn represents balance and Libra is dance, the most desirable quality for dance is balance, it requires perfect balance. Everything on this earth is perfectly balanced and the dance of 'Nataraja' is going on continuously and the whole nature is presenting that dance that is perfectly balanced. Lord Saturn keeps balancing everything.

Libra is the marketplace and Saturn is honesty. The exaltation of Saturn indicates that the person will be honest in doing business. Exalted Saturn indicates that one will give an equal share to all without any bias. Libra is a symbol of companionship, Librans are generous and help others, Saturn is respect, partnership will last long when you respect and help your partner. It indicates that the person will listen to the opinion of the public at large and will give importance to everyone's opinion and then will make a final decision, no one can influence the decision taken by Saturn. Aries represents single nature, while Libra represents partnership, these two zodiac signs are opposite to each other. Aries represents the singular soul and Saturn rules the masses. The element of Aries does not support the nature of Saturn and it becomes debilitated in this sign.

The position of Saturn in the horoscope indicates delay and struggle in matters related to the respective house, but Saturn always fulfills his promises. The transit of Saturn brings changes in the life of a person. Saturn has the power to destroy all material desires of a person and shows the true picture of life that only death is certain in this world, a very strong Saturn makes a person a hermit.

Affliction: If Saturn is afflicted the native will become lethargic, idle, lazy. It indicates denial, depression, disharmony, disappointment, dejection, despondency, a difference of opinion, etc. If it is heavily afflicted the native will become a cruel criminal. This creates distortion and paranoia. Saturn is dark, afflicted Saturn indicates underworld activities, sexual perversions, and unnatural sexual activities. The native will do any harm to others for the fulfillment of his desire. The native feels pleasure by causing pain to others and will use any kind of violence.

Body Parts and diseases: Hair and its growth, teeth, bladder, muscles, wrist, feet. Disease: Injury, operation, fracture, gallstone, anaemia, dryness, numbness, paralysis, muscular pain, toothache, joint pains, etc.

4.8 The Lunar Nodes - Rahu and Ketu

According to mythology, Lord Vishnu beheaded a demon named Swarnabhanu while he was sitting by the side of the gods at the time of distributing amrita (nectar). At that time, Swarnabhanu knew that the gods were not going to fulfill their promise of equitable distribution of nectar. He changed his entire outfit, began to look like a deity, and sat on the side where the deity was sitting to drink the nectar. But Sun and Moon recognized him that he is not a deity, he is a demon and they informed Lord Vishnu. Immediately Lord Vishnu beheaded him but before that, he had drunk a few drops of nectar. That's why he became immortal. His head is called Rahu and his headless body becomes Ketu. The energy of these nodes is strange and mysterious and they always move in retrograde motion.

In Indian astrology Sun, Earth and Moon; three planets are involved to create the energy of Rahu and Ketu. The ecliptic is an imaginary line on the sky that marks the annual path of the Sun. The movement of the Earth and the Moon on their path produces enormous energy. The motion of the Moon when intersects this path, disturbs this energy. When the Moon's orbit crosses the ecliptic to the north, that point of intersection is called Rahu. Ketu is the point 180° apart from that intersection. Thus, Rahu and Ketu are the two imaginary points without any shape. This intersection creates the disturbance of two massive energies, any planet near these nodes gets disturbed and creates unusual events in the life of the native.

When a planet in transit crosses these nodes in the birth chart, there is a disturbance in the matter related to the respective house.

Some scriptures say that Rahu is exalted in Taurus and debilitated in Scorpio and Ketu is vice-versa. While some other classics say that Rahu is exalted in Gemini and debilitated in Sagittarius. Rahu is the co-ruler of Aquarius and its Mooltrikona sign is Virgo, while Ketu is the co-ruler of Scorpio and its Mooltrikona sign is Pisces. Both nodes represent tall in height and age of 100 years.

4.8.1 Rahu

Rahu - the north node of the Moon is a shadowy planet. The direction of Rahu is South-West and stays 18 months in a sign. The caste of Rahu is Malechha (outcaste) and it represents all foreign elements like a foreign land, foreign caste, foreign people, etc. Rahu represents those reptiles having poison in their mouths like snakes, while Ketu represents those insects and creatures having poison in tails like scorpions. Rahu's gemstone is Gomedha.

The above mythology is very important to understand the characteristic of Rahu. Like Swarnabhanu had an intense desire to drink the nectar at any cost. Rahu signifies passion and obsession. To achieve this burning desire, he changed his face, his clothes, left the side of demons, joined the side of devatas, and took big risks with only one goal or better we can say with only one obsession – "I want this nectar at any cost" and he achieved it. But after achieving this, he lost his body shape.

The behavior of the person having a strong influence on Rahu is also the same. They are extremely obsessed to achieve their desire. For that purpose, they can cross any limits and don't care about the outcome and suffering. Just as Swarnabhanu lost the shape of his body in the end, similarly a person following the path of his obsession has to lose a lot from his life. One day he will get what he wants but for that, he will have to pay a very high price, like Swarnabhanu paid the price.

Mythology says that the Sun and the Moon recognized the demon sitting by the side of the gods and informed Lord Vishnu. After that, Sun and Moon became strong enemies of Rahu and Ketu, eclipse caused due to the transit of Rahu & Ketu and they have complete power to engulf Sun and Moon.

Sun and Moon represent our soul and mind. It means that if you run after your materialistic desire your soul and mind will become weak, your vision will become blurred and you will not be able to identify the truth. The smoke of materialism will gradually surround you and it will take over your soul and mind. But if your soul and mind are strong then you can recognize the illusion created by Rahu. The person who has strong Sun and Moon in his horoscope can easily catch the hidden motive of the mischievous persons and keep himself away from all these. This is one of the many reasons, we worship the Sun and the Moon in Hindu culture so that our spirit and mind are strong and not eclipsed by material desire in the mundane world.

Rahu has only a mouth but no body. It indicates that a person with a strong influence of Rahu has a great desire but does not have the ability to digest it. Rahu always thinks about the future and its position in the horoscope indicates that the person wants to experience things that he does not have till now. Rahu means imbalance, mistakes; Where a person learns from his experience. The Rahu-Ketu axis reflects the karmic balance that we carry from our past lives – what we did and what we want to achieve.

Rahu is such a power that does not listen to anyone's advice and is ready to cross any limit to fulfill his intense desire. Such natives do not care about the result, even if their head is cut off like Swarnabhanu.

Rahu is an airy and lawless planet. Rahu does not like any boundaries. A person having a strong influence of Rahu behaves the same. They don't want any control over themselves, they are ready to break any rule, and sometimes their behavior is over expansive. They don't like any questions and they don't want to give any explanations. They wander here and there like air and waste their time and energy.

Rahu indicates name, fame, overnight popularity, glamour, media sensation, material success, etc. All these represent illusion to the material world, and Rahu is the lord of all illusion. Due to the effect of Rahu, the person will show his face to the world and become popular. It controls the film and cinema industry, advertising industry, all modern computers, television, etc., and those jobs where a person is showing their face to the masses.

Rahu represents smoke, materialism, drugs, dark, and poison. Rahu is subtle, insensitive, deceptive, telling lies, harsh and voluptuous planet. Malefic Rahu indicates the person who will not think even twice of betraying his most trusted person. He can go to any extent to fulfill his desire.

Rahu represents paternal grandfather, quarrelsome person, greediness, cunningness, conspiracy, modern technology, foreigners, skin diseases, indigestion, restlessness, swelling in the body, problem-related with gas, black magic, phobias, gambling, speculation, leprosy, giddiness, fear from unknow, insanity, smuggling, underworld activities, terrorists, etc.

4.8.2 Ketu

Ketu - the south node, is the shadow planet of sudden and unexpected things. It also represents the experiences of our past lives, which we learned at a very high level and with mastery. It also represents a rigid and critical mindset where perfection is the highest goal at any cost. Ketu gemstone is Cat's eye also known as Lehsunia.

The symbol of Ketu is a flag that always stands vertically indicating the direction of the planet. A flag represents victory, but victory is not easy, victory on the battlefield is followed by great bloodshed and great sacrifices. The position of Ketu indicates that the native will get a victory after a lot of hard work and great sacrifice. Ketu provides clairvoyance and wisdom but after sufferings.

A strong Ketu blessed the native with powerful insights. It gives a power of intense concentration and deep penetration. This also represents vaccination where medicine is injected into the body. Ketu represents strong intuition, isolation, mediation, deep research, scientific jobs, drilling activities, etc. It belongs to those jobs where a person does with full concentration, to achieve their goal the person leaves the rest of the world and forgets everything. A strong Ketu is necessary to sit in the meditation for long hours. Ketu is a planet of seclusion and has no interest in the material world, the higher aspect of Ketu is salvation (Moksha).

Ketu represents inertia and strong attachment towards the past. It also represents a tendency where people want to live in their own world and do not want to change anything. Ketu also represents Infra-Red Light, which is also not visible to human eyes represents the mysterious functioning of this planet. It belongs to those diseases that are hidden and not easy to identify.

Ketu denotes separation, in which Ketu is placed it indicates separation from all materialistic things related to that house. Ketu is a planet of sudden events; a person has to face sudden changes in his life related to the matter of the concerned house. A malefic Ketu represents false sainthood, false knowledge, cheating, and humbugging profession, jealousy, hatred, deceit, murder, low-class sinful habits, etc. These nodes indicate all hidden criminal, anti-social activities that are done mostly at night.

4.9 Difference in Desire of Mars and Rahu

Mars is desire, and Rahu is also desire. Due to Martian energy, we move in this world and run behind our desire. So, what is the difference between these two desires?

Mars is a push. When a person runs behind his desire and utilizes his energy in a positive way, such desire is Martian. One works hard to fulfill such desire. But when a person does not want to work hard and wants to fulfill his desire by immoral means, that is Rahu.

Rahu is a criminal, Rahu is an illusion, Rahu is deceit, Rahu is an obsession, and Rahu does not want to listen to anyone's advice. Remember the story of Samudra Manthan (Churning the Ocean), Swarnabhanu wanted the nectar at any cost and he is not afraid of any punishment and cutting his head. He wanted to fulfill that desire by hook or by crook and he achieved that, but later he paid a very high price of separation of his head from his body. The chopped-off head of the Swarnabhanu is the final result of Rahu's obsession.

For example, if a student is working hard to clear an exam, he is utilizing Martian energy in a constructive manner. While another student is using deceitful methods to clear it, that is Rahu.

A person is working hard to get money, so he is improving his skills, such is Martian desire (a push to achieve something), while the other person decides to cheat people, indulge in fraudulent activities, indulge in theft and robbery, all such desires and activities are Rahu.

A person is looking for a promotion and to achieve such desire he starts working hard, he is improving his skills, he is learning new software, he is putting his Martian energy to achieve such an objective. On the other hand, there is another person who is using flattery to get a promotion rather than improving his skills. He starts using unethical means to fulfill his desire, that is Rahu.

Like Swarnabhanu had changed his face and even demi-gods were unable to recognize him, other than the Sun and the Moon. The person influenced with Rahu will change his face several times to fulfill his desire, and every face looks so real that it is very difficult to recognize such person's real face. Rahu has only one objective – "I want to fulfill this desire at any cost, and I am not afraid if my head is cut off for the fulfillment of such purpose." Remember, Rahu has no limit, he can cross any limit to fulfill his desire.

Rahu is temptation and false attraction. Rahu knows that my wish will not come true if I tell the truth. So, he always shows a rosy picture which attracts the temptation of the person. Rahu makes false promises, in fact, he does not care about promises, and he only cares about the achievement of his objective. The words spoken by Rahu have no meaning; he can turn at any time. But Mars is loyal, committed and never makes false promises.

Rahu always laughs how clever he is in deceiving others, how he fools others on false promises. But if Mars is unable to fulfill a promise, he regrets it and immediately says sorry to that person.

Rahu wants to enjoy on the wealth and misery of others, and will fight how not to give. But Mars, the sibling of Earth will never enjoy the wealth of others, and just as Earth has the quality of giving, Mars has the same quality. He returns the others possessions with full honesty.

Mars is the protector, who uses his force and weapon always for protection. But Rahu always uses his power only for the fulfillment of his desire. Mars is ready to sacrifice himself for others, Rahu is also not afraid of death but, only to fulfill his desire and never do any sacrifice.

Rahu is not afraid of dying and being killed, but his purpose must be served. But Mars, the protector will leave the path if he finds that the purpose is wrong.

Mars always thinks about others to protect and is ready to give. Rahu never thinks about others and is always ready to snatch from others.

When a person uses Martian energy to fulfill his desire, which is a constructive path, he feels rejoices and shows his achievement to others. When a person uses Rahu's energy to fulfill his desire, immediately after getting the desired object he disappears. Others come to know his true face only when his desires are fulfilled.

Chapter 5

Depression

When a person reaches his middle age and the slow-moving planets start making a hard aspect on their natal position, then the situation in life gradually starts changing. Tension and conflict in life gradually increase with each passing day and the person does not understand why one after the other problem is coming. But such a situation does not change immediately and gradually the person starts losing his fighting spirit and his hope too.

A general feeling of anxiety is acceptable because it is normal for human behaviour but when it lasts for a long time which starts to affect the mental and physical health of the person, it is not normal and can be a symptom of depression.

I have seen that the problem of depression does not come in the life of every person who has gone through a midlife crisis. It comes only for those who have such specific combinations in their horoscope. If there are some negative combinations in the birth chart, then the person may face the problem of depression and sometimes it can remain for a long time. There is no relation between depression and midlife crisis but if such combinations exist in a chart, then during the mid-life crisis the situation becomes very bad and the person starts taking depression pills.

Here the question arises whether astrology can help in such matters or not. With the help of astrology, we can know which planets and their conjunction is putting pressure on the native. Whether the person has such type of combinations in his birth chart or it is happening due to transit of any malefic planet.

If there are malefic combinations then astrology can help the person to overcome such situation and if it is happening due to transit of any malefic planet then the person can know the timing of transit and take precautionary measures till the transit is affected.

5.1 Important Role of Planets

The Sun, The Moon, and Mercury play an important role as it controls our soul, mind, and intellect. The strength of these planets decides how a person will fight when the situation turns against him in his life. If these planets are weak, badly placed, conjunct, or aspect by malefic planets like Saturn, Mars, Rahu, and Ketu and no aspect of any benefic planets, then there is a strong possibility that the person starts feeling frustrated very soon and he will lose his fighting spirit. The reason for going into such a condition could be any; Family matters, problems in marriage, problems in the profession, job loss, financial matters, etc. The dasha and antardasha of the planets play an important role and if Venus antardasha starts under Saturn Mahadasha then such period is very tough for the native.

5.1.1 The Sun, The Moon, and Mercury

(Discussed in Chapter 4: The Planets)

5.1.2 Weak Moon

A debilitated and badly placed Moon may lead the native into depression very easily. Mildness, kindness, love, affection is presented by the Moon and if it is afflicted then the native may lack such tender qualities. If Moon is placed in any Ketu ruled nakshatra (Ashwini, Magha, Mula) then the person nature is very impulsive. If the malefics effects are more on the native, then the person may take sudden and serious action.

An afflicted Moon makes the native over anxious, indecisive, rash, depressed, and pessimistic. Following are the important conditions related with the weak Moon;

- Moon is considered weak up to 72 degrees from either side of Sun. Such a Moon if conjunct or aspect by malefic planet like Sun, Saturn, Mars and Rahu / Ketu, then, person gets easily frustrated.

- If Moon is hemmed between two or more malefic planets. For example, in chart 1 in chapter 3, Moon is placed in first house, Saturn is placed in second house and Rahu is placed in 12th house. Such Moon is hemmed between Saturn and Rahu.

- If Moon is situated alone in the chart and no planet is situated on either side of the Moon.

Also, the person's dilemma level is high and unable to take decisions, if Moon is placed in any water sign (Cancer, Scorpio and Pisces). An afflicted and weak Moon in these signs can lead the person into frustration very easily and the person is not able to decide what to do, what actions he should take!

5.2 Houses

Astrology has divided the entire space into 12 equal sections. These sections are called Houses or Bhavas (in Sanskrit) means – "Birth, coming into existence". Earth is moving on its axis from West to East and due to its rotation, we can see only one part of the sky at a time. The zodiac moves one after the other towards the horizon, changing every two hours and rising again in the east about 24 hours later. Each bhava has its own meaning and the result of each bhava changes continuously due to the transit of celestial bodies.

The planets ruling the sign are called lord or owner of the house and the planet situated on the sign is a tenant of that house. The strength of the ruling planet is important for the optimum functioning of the house, but the final conclusion will be taken only after the consideration of – the owner, the tenant and aspect of other planets. If the house is vacant, it does not mean that it is worthless, rather it means that there is no tenant (planet) and only the owner of the house is responsible for all the matters related to them including aspect of other planets.

For depression 1ˢᵗ house, 4ᵗʰ house and 5ᵗʰ house and placement of their lord are very important.

5.2.1 The 1st House

Ascendant is called the first house of the horoscope, is the sign of the zodiac which is rising on the eastern horizon at the time of birth. The zodiac sign falling on the ascendant and the planets situated on them decide the physical structure of the person. The first house is the house of self. It represents birth, the soul has got a physical body. This physical body contains all the qualities, general appearance, prominent traits, colour, shape, and other characteristics related to the first house. It represents the individual's urges and his orientation towards life in this material world.

This house represents the energy, vitality, general disposition, health, and span of life. If the house is strong, then the person is courageous enough to face any difficulty in life. He is determined and does not waver from difficult circumstances. The first house represents head and brain, name, fame, dignity, self-respect, beauty, prestige, happiness, concern, longevity, etc.

Affliction: A weak first house creates mental tension and lack of vitality. When afflicted, weakness and other health-related problems are also seen from here.

5.2.2 The 4th House

The 4th house relates to the Moon. It represents our emotions, sensitivity, psychology, heart, dreams, and desires. This is the house of the mother and represents our early childhood education. This is the house of our home and family – the family which we create in this world. It represents happiness, peace, and the domestic environment. The atmosphere of the family is good if this house is strong and receives good aspects. This house is also considered a 'Grave' which represents all hidden things and secret affairs of the native.

This is the house of the masses and indicates the popularity of the person. This house indicates vehicles and conveyances, houses, movable and immovable property, leased or rented property, real estate, land, comforts, and luxuries. Where the lord of the fourth house is situated, the person will seek happiness in the matter related to that house.

Affliction: An afflicted 4th house indicates; physical ailments of the breast and chest, mental disorder, problems in the lungs, lunacy, and problem related to the circulatory system. It is the most sensitive house and afflictions indicate a lack of peace.

5.2.3 The 5th House

This is the house of our creativity which takes place at different levels of manifestation. It is the house of the fruits of our efforts that manifest in time. The relation of the fifth house with the Kendra houses is very auspicious and provides good results. This is the house of our children – creativity manifests on the physical plane. This is the house of love affairs and the planets in this house indicate how we show our love to others.

This is the house of worship, religion, wisdom, intelligence, knowledge, mantras, and intuition. This house is known as "Poorva Punya Sthana" i.e., good deeds from our previous birth". All our hobbies and creativities are nothing but the accumulation of all our deeds. When we pour some water on the surface, it dries up after some time, but when we pour water again, it follows the same path where the water disappeared earlier. In this way our "Karma i.e., Deeds" compels us to act in this material world, which the 5th house represents.

This house belongs to our abdomen, entertainment, sports, speculation, gambling, creative arts, traditional laws, ancient literature, advisory, change in job and profession, learning, and teaching. The location of the 5th lord indicates that the native likes to work on matters related to that house.

Affliction: An afflicted fifth house or its lord indicates problem in knowledge, wisdom, talent, creative intelligence, natural inclinations etc.

Any connection between these houses with 6th, 8th and 12th houses or its lords, placement of malefic planets among these houses along with badly afflicted Moon makes the person easily depressed.

5.3 The Eclipse

Eclipse plays a major role to put a person into depression. It causes a serious impact on the life of the native, especially if the Sun and the Moon are in the same house with Rahu or Ketu. If the conjunction between these two nodes is less than five degrees then the intensity would be severe. The effect of a solar eclipse is more severe than a lunar eclipse, if there is any such conjunction in a horoscope, although not every eclipse is harmful to a person with this type of conjunction. It depends on which constellation the eclipse is taking place.

If there is any malefic conjunction in your horoscope or your natal moon is weak, then try to remain calm during the eclipse. I have noticed that two weeks before and after the eclipse, the level of disturbance in such people becomes very high.

Example 1:

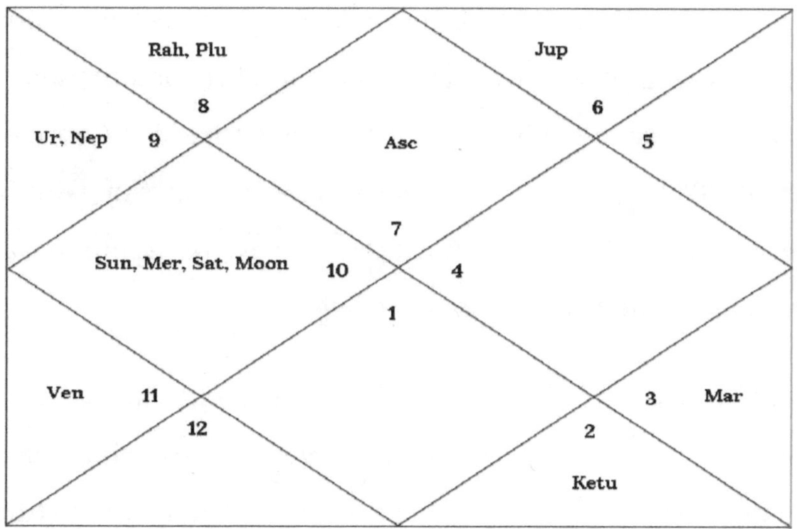

Asc.-Libra-10:52:21

Sun-Capricorn-10:02:18

Moon-Capricorn-21:18:22

Saturn-Capricorn-25:08:20

This case is of a person born in the year January 1993. His Sun is situated in Capricorn at 10° 02' 18" and Moon is also in 21° 18' 22" Capricorn which is the fourth house of the horoscope. The difference between these two luminaires is 11° 16' 4" which is less than 72° and it is a new moon day (the difference is less than 13.2°). Saturn is also situated there and aspecting 6th house, 10th house and ascendant.

Moon represents our mind and moonlight (difference between the Sun and the Moon) represents strength of mind. Lack of moonlight indicates a room where light is less, then the person in the room feels afraid due to darkness and get panic soon. Here the room is our mind where there is no light (it is a new moon day), so such a person will easily panic in difficult situations of life. The worrisome point is Saturn is also situated at Capricorn at 25° 8' 20", which is making a very close conjunction with the Moon. This person is prone to diseases, feels immediate nervousness and over-anxious.

When Saturn started transiting in Capricorn, it started many problems in the life of the native. However, the auspicious planet Jupiter is aspecting the fourth house which is providing protection to the person.

Example 2:

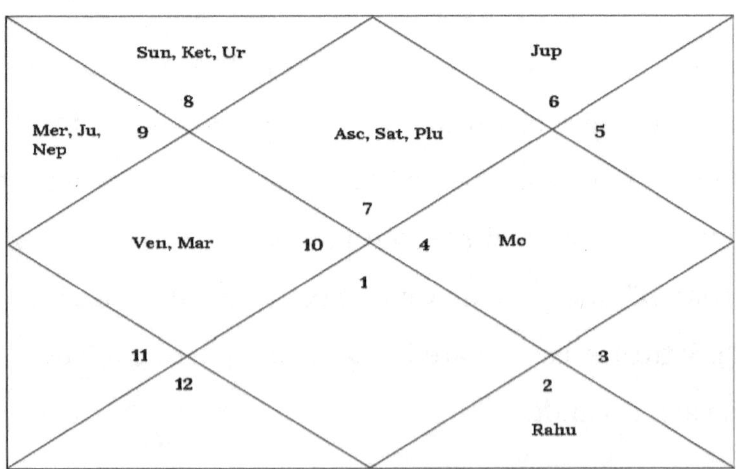

Asc.- Libra-04:29:36   Sun -Scorpio -26:23:20
Moon - Cancer - 07:59:16   Saturn-Libra-29:02:10

This is the chart of a female born in the year December 1984. In this case, ascendant lord Venus is situated in 4th house with Mars. Saturn is the lord of the 4th and 5th house which is situated in the ascendant. The situation in the life of the native starts changing when Saturn entered in Capricorn. Saturn is transiting over the ascendant lord Venus and is aspecting the Moon from its 7th aspect (opposition). Hence, during such time situation starts changing at home and the workplace. The problem was aggravated when Ketu entered Scorpio in September 2020. The second house is the house of savings and Ketu is a planet of separation, starts separating from savings. When Ketu exit from Scorpio in April 2022, then situation starts getting normal.

It is difficult to change the destiny, but such information will help us to utilize the time is a constructive manner and do not feel panic when tide turns against in our life. We patiently cross such period and utilize the time for our inner development. Such knowledge will help us to take preventive measures in advance. It is sure to rain, if we have an umbrella we can avoid getting wet.

Example 3:

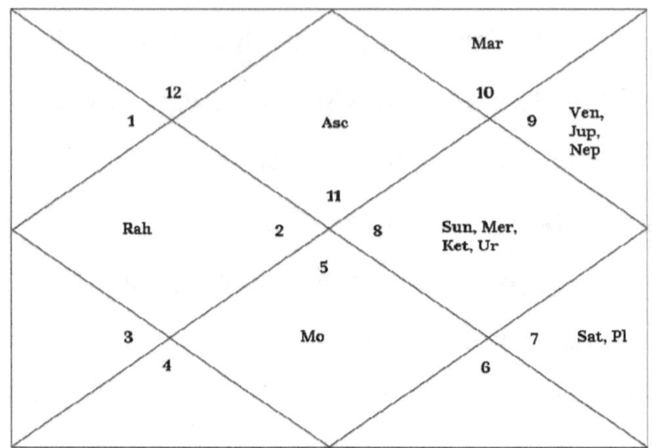

Asc.-Aquarius-12:50:59   Sun-Scorpio-02:30:50
Moon-Leo-29:05:25   Saturn-Libra-26:18:16

The above case pertains to the person whose birth year is November 1984. In this chart, Ketu along with Sun is situated in Anuradha Nakshatra in Scorpio. On 26 May 2021, there was a lunar eclipse in the constellation of Anuradha. That time Moon was in Anuradha Nakshatra and was in close proximity with Ketu causing eclipse. The circumstances suddenly change in the life of the native, which put him in depression. However, after six months he finds himself able to overcome such a situation.

Eclipse plays an important role and brings about many important changes in the life of the native, if it falls in the same Nakshatra and has proximity with the planets of birth.

Note: In the above examples, these natives have not yet attained their middle age. But there was a problem of despair and depression in their life. However, if such transits and events affect the person during his mid-life then the situation may become more serious.

Chapter 6

Transit of Planets

A horoscope is a snapshot of the sky when a person is born. The zodiac signs that rise and set at the time and the planetary positions in them, guide the life path of the person. But the planets are not fixed, they keep on moving and transiting through different signs. This transit produces different types of energy. Although the effect of the transiting planet is temporary in our life and when the planet moves out of the sign, the energy level changes, and then its effect also changes.

We can understand the planets in the birth chart as mother and father, who always have an impact on us, no matter how old we become. The transiting planet is like our class teacher, when we study in class 1st then our class teacher has full right to punish us, but when we leave the class and study in the higher classes, then the authority goes to that class teacher. Similarly, the transiting planet affects us as long as it remains in that sign. When it leaves and some other planet comes then the right to influence us goes to the newcomer. But what we got from our parents affects our whole life, in the same way, the planets of birth affect us throughout life.

Transit provides us with useful information about upcoming changes in energy levels and favorable and unfavorable times. The information guides us to channelize our energy in the right direction, make better use of available resources, and take necessary measures on gloomy days. This information also destroys the person's ego and despair, that there is a higher energy working behind us, as a human we only have to do our work, and "I did" the attachment to the word disappears. We have to sow only good seeds, fruits will come when the time turns favourable.

Every planet in our solar system rotates around the Sun and the time of one rotation is different for each planet. The transit effect of slow-moving planets – Jupiter, Saturn, Rahu, and Uranus create significant changes during midlife and their effects are longer than that of fast-moving planets.

Jupiter stays in a sign for a year, Saturn stays in a sign for 2.5 years, Rahu and Ketu stay in a sign for 1.5 years, and Uranus stays in a sign for 7 years. Many life-changing events take place during this transit which affects the person deeply.

Jupiter, Venus, unafflicted Mercury, and Moon (more than 72 degrees) are considered benefic planets. While transiting they produce favorable results when they conjoin or make aspects with the position of planets in our natal chart. Sun, Mars, Saturn, Rahu, and Ketu are considered malefic and produce unfavorable results when they conjoin or make aspects with the planets in our horoscope.

When a benefic planet transits in its favourable signs and conjoins or makes an aspect with a benefic planet then it produces favorable results and vice-versa. Jupiter's most favorable sign is cancer, therefore, when Jupiter transit through cancer most favorable results are possible, while Saturn's most detrimental sign is also cancer, when Saturn transits into cancer many life-changing events happen.

While the aspect of malefic planets creates trouble in life, the aspect of benefic planets provides a cushion to the native.

In this chapter, we will discuss only the transit of – Jupiter, Saturn, Rahu, Uranus, and Neptune as they are responsible for the midlife crisis.

6.1 The Transit of Jupiter

Jupiter completes one rotation around the Sun in 12 years and stays in a sign for a year. After every 12 years Jupiter transit over its natal position and completes a cycle. Such transit brings significant changes in the life of the person.

When Jupiter transit over its natal position the level of energy in the significant house becomes strong. Therefore, the person takes much interest in the activities related to the house and the concerning sign. The age of - 12, 24, 36, 48, 60, etc. are important years in life when a person leaves their past activities or past engagements and start a new activity. Such conjunction at these years is the beginning of a new cycle in life.

During midlife, Jupiter starts making opposition aspect with its natal position at the age of 42 years (3.5 cycles of the zodiac completed). The square aspect of the natal position at the age of 45 years (3.75 cycles of the zodiac completed), and conjunction to its natal position at the age of 48 years (completed 4 cycles of the zodiac).

Jupiter is considered a planet of fortune and its transit brings remarkable changes in life. Its transit and aspects bring luck and happiness in life. However, the planet of luck also creates obstacles when it forms hard aspects in the horoscope. Then the person wanders here and there with no fruitful outcome. Jupiter controls liver, sugar, fat, hips, thighs, circulation of blood in the arteries, pancreas, etc. in the body. When Jupiter creates a hard aspect, the person may suffer from sugar, liver-related problem, flatulence, etc. in his life at the age of about 42 years.

Jupiter's transit and aspects change the perception of the person towards his life. Many people start taking interest in religious activities after the age of 42. Due to hard aspects, the planet of wisdom changes the belief of the person. Those who were once skeptics and agnostics at a young age begin to believe in religion and many of them take interest in literature who have never studied a book before. Many of them start worshiping and they like to study subjects like astrology, palmistry, homeopathy, etc.

The transit of Jupiter makes a person think about what he has done so far and what is the meaning of the goals that he had set at his young age at the beginning of his journey. The planet of direction brings the person's life in a direction; However, the method of teaching is hard at this time.

6.2 The Transit of Saturn

Saturn completes one rotation around the Sun in almost 30 years and stays in a sign for 2.5 years. After every 30 years, Saturn transit in its natal position and completes half its cycle in 15 years.

The tough master Saturn's transit brings limitations, restrictions, delays, and misfortunes during midlife when it makes a hard aspect to the Sun, the Moon, Ascendant, and MC (10th house).

When Saturn transits or aspect the natal Sun, problems arise in life with father, superiors, and officials. Saturn is a challenger, so subordinates will challenge their superiors if they are being suppressed for a long time and unable to speak. Saturn ruling the working class will provide such power and such a transit will change the scenario in life forever.

Saturn's transit over Moon brings problems with mother, depression, and mental agony. Saturn's transit over Venus brings trouble with the wife, female relatives, and scandals. There is also the possibility of financial gains during such a transit. Saturn's transit over Mars brings quarrels and accidents, its transit over Jupiter brings financial gains and the start of a new venture, success in investments; its transit over Mercury brings trouble through documents, also increased interest in literature and study; Saturn's transit over natal Saturn brings significant changes in life and it put questions on everything that the person has done till now is his life.

Saturn creates an opposition aspect to its natal position at the age of 45 years and completes a 1.5 cycle of rotation. The opposition aspect creates struggle and tension because there is a lack of harmony between these two energies.

When hard aspect form to Ascendant, Sun, Moon, and MC simultaneously then the condition becomes more serious, for some time in life everything seems to be stalled, such a transit blocks the movement of energy. Remember, Saturn stays in a sign for 2.5 years and start affecting the next sign before 6 months of its actual transit. Therefore, this problem can remain in the life of the native for about three years.

Saturn means balance and discipline. The tough master teaches one to be balanced, it destroys one's ego and reflects the real truth of life.

6.3 The Transit of Rahu and Ketu

Rahu and Ketu always move retrograde and complete one cycle in 18 years and stay in a sign for 1.5 years. The behavior of both these nodes is sudden, so when they change their sign unexpected events happen. The event triggered by them can affect the native for 1.5 years as they stay in that zodiac during that period.

Rahu creates hard aspects during midlife and catches the person for 1.5 years. At the age of 45, Rahu makes an opposite aspect from its natal position and completes 2.5 cycles. Such an aspect creates conflict and gives birth to unexpected events.

However, Ketu has no aspect, therefore, it does not create any hard aspect. It is responsible only for those matters related to the house in which it enters during transit.

The shadow planet Rahu is considered a curtain. At our home curtain prevents the sunlight from coming into the room and the room becomes slightly darker. When Rahu transit over the natal Sun then the sunlight becomes dim or when Rahu comes in front of the natal Sun then it works as a curtain and prevents sunlight from coming into that house. Due to the absence of sunlight, the problem related to the house starts which can last for 1.5 years.

After every 18 years, these two nodes return to the same position in the natal chart, then many significant changes happen in the life of the person. Rahu represents hunger and Ketu represents separation. These two nodes represent disturbed energies, where the nodes are placed the matter related to the house is always disturbed. The house in which, they are located in the birth chart, after 18 years when they return over there, the energy level would become high and unexpected events may happen related to the house concerned.

6.4 The Transit of Uranus

The transit of Uranus affects the life of every person and it happens only once when Uranus makes an opposite aspect from its natal position at the age of 42 years. After crossing such age, Uranus makes an angle of 180 degrees from its birth position. Therefore, after 42 years, many important changes start in the life of a person.

Uranus is the seventh planet from the Sun and completes its orbit every 84 years and stays in a zodiac for 7 years. Therefore, after every 7 years, various harmonic changes take place in the life of a person. At the age of 42, Uranus crosses six signs from its natal position and completes its half cycle.

Every planet in our solar system rotates on its axis with a tilt, like Earth is titled 23.5°, and Mars is tilted at 24°. But the axial tilt of Uranus is 97.7°. Therefore, one pole of the planet constantly faces the Sun while the other faces away. The result is an unusual cycle of day and night at the poles and one day lasts for 42 years followed by night for 42 years.

Uranus is exalted at 23° in Scorpio and debilitated in Taurus. Scorpio is the sign of transformation. It is the darkest of all the constellations and is related to hidden aspects of life. Uranus represents unconventional matters in life. It represents freedom from tradition and an urge towards differentiation. Uranus doesn't like anything orthodoxical and prefers to do things in its own way.

Uranus gives strength to break the old rules and the person prefers to find their own path in life. The house in which the planet is situated the person doesn't like to follow the boundaries and always thinks about doing something other. Like, if Uranus is placed in Sagittarius, then the person doesn't like to follow the rules of religion and thinks of changing the old beliefs. If Sagittarius sign falls in the second house, then the person doesn't like to follow the tradition of his family. The second house also represents savings, the person doesn't like to follow the traditional path of saving like doing a 9 to 5 job, and doesn't want anyone to control his savings. The transit of Uranus takes a person closer to his destiny.

After the age of 42 years, the cycle starts to change but every change has to go through a transition phase and such a transition is not only related to career and money but it can be your relationship, health, business, etc. Like, night turns into day and day turns into the night but it happens gradually and in between, there is a period of transition. So, after 42 years the transition phase in life begins. The opposition aspect creates pressure to change the old beliefs. There is a strong urge to change the traditional path and the person starts questioning the work he has done so far. He starts thinking of doing something else in life and starts exploring new activities.

Uranus's behaviour is sudden; therefore, the person witnesses sudden changes in life at this time and the boundaries which he is thinking of breaking many times, and now he is ready to take action. The person may suddenly change their career path and start doing something other which may be an unconventional path.

Suppose, a person has a desire to start his own venture but he hesitates to leave the job. When everything seems good in life and when such an aspect starts, suddenly the person may be fired from the organization or the person may continue to work but simultaneously he starts working to establish his own venture. The opposite aspect creates pressure and Uranus starts creating differentiation, such a person cannot smoothly continue his work. Uranus forces the person to work as per the desire of his soul. The planet that doesn't want to follow the conventional path pulls the person towards his destiny.

Uranus teaches us that the path of uniqueness and unconventional is better without which there are no changes in life. But it is a such powerful energy that requires proper direction.

Uranus forces the person to introspect what you have done so far and what your soul desires. It is better to accept the change when the situation demands it and not resist. The mid-life crisis opens up a new horizon, although it is not a cakewalk. The completion of the half cycle of Uranus is the beginning of a new chapter in life.

Such an opposing aspect also calls for a change in dietary habits as our body has completed half its cycle of replacement with a new set of cells.

The opposite aspect works as if the person is looking at the other side of the coin. The truth of life which you have not experienced till now begins to unfold in front of you. The transit of Uranus brings major upheaval in a person's life. It forces a person to set new goals for his life by looking at both sides of the coin.

After 84 years one cycle of Uranus is completed and a group of people with Uranus in the same zodiac gets separated. Therefore, the influence of this planet is mainly generational.

6.5 The Transit of Neptune

Neptune, the cold, blue, gas giant planet is the eighth planet from the Sun. Of the three outer planets, it is the second one and represents Maya or illusion in astrology. Neptune bestows the person with intuition, inspiration, kindness, and compassion. It is the planet of our subconscious and represents dreams, fantasies, and addiction. Neptune completes one cycle of rotation around the Sun in 164 years and stays in a sign for almost 14 years. The transit of Neptune brings changes in the life of the person to see the things in reality and rise above illusion to a higher level of spirituality.

Illusion means what is not real seems to be true. The manifestation of illusion is very strong in this mundane world and without the understanding of Maya (illusion), a person cannot raise his level of consciousness. On the higher aspect, the transit of Neptune makes the person spiritual and provides an in-depth vision to understand the cycle of Maya. But it is possible only when the person has seen phases of illusion in his life. The illusion created in one's mind about something provides energy to move in this mundane world. To get that the person runs behind that object.

Neptune represents hope, happiness, and the movement towards the attainment of the desired object. However, the real truth will come later. It represents understanding through experience which ultimately takes the individual to a higher level of spirituality.

At the age of 42, Neptune completes 90 degrees of the zodiac in the birth chart and makes a square aspect to its natal position.

The journey of life is full of dreams at the beginning, the planet of dreams and illusion shows the rosy picture and raises hopes.

But when it completes 90 degrees of the zodiac in the natal chart of the person, that person's eyes are not blurred, because he has burnt his fingers by walking on those rosy paths.

A midlife crisis opens a new horizon in the life of the person. The dreams you have chosen at a young age are very superficial because you are aware of only one side of the coin. Such a hard aspect of Neptune has shattered all those dreams and forced you to see the other side of the coin.

The midlife crisis is just the beginning of the second part of the journey in life.

The Timing of Midlife Crisis

Planets	Time to Complete One Revolution Around the Sun	Stay in a Sign	Cycle Completed By Midlife	Transit to Natal (Years)	
	(Years)	(Years)		Opposition Aspect	Square Aspect
Jupiter	12	1	3.5	42	45
Saturn	30	2.5	1.5	45	
Rahu	18	1.5	2.5	45	
Uranus	84	7	0.5	42	
Neptune	168	14	0.25		42

6.6 Progression Chart

Progression Chart plays an important role for doing predictions and without such analysis the final interpretation may be wrong. Progression chart is prepared for a year and it requires the native's date of birth, time, place and the present date.

Birth chart is the snapshot of the sky but planets are continuously moving. A progressed chart shows how far the planets have moved till date from the position of the natal chart. During midlife progressed Ascendant, MC, Sun and Moon form hard aspects to the natal position and activated between the age of 42 to 49 years. Such aspects make the situation more severe and it could lead to major financial loss, major health issues or danger to life during that year.

In order to understand the proper situation of the native, it is necessary to study the birth chart as well as the progress chart. However, the calculations of this chart are beyond the preview of this book.

Example 4:

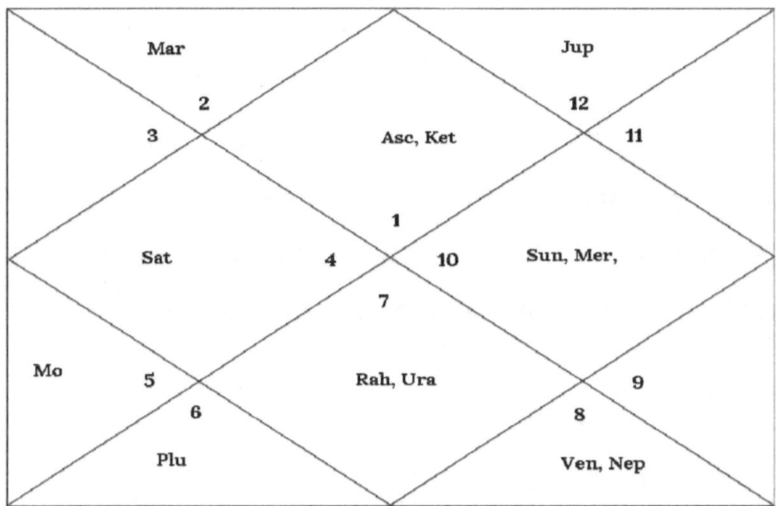

Asc.-Aries-16:08:08   Sun-Capricorn-05:48:49
Moon-Leo-16:50:30   Saturn-Cancer-06:05:43

This is the case of the person born in the year January 1976. At the age of 44 years, Saturn entered in Capricorn which is his 10th house and his natal Sun is also there. Natal Saturn is situated in 4th house which sign is Cancer. On 24 Jan 2020, Saturn entered in Capricorn and formed a conjunction with natal Sun, square aspect with ascendant, and opposition aspect with natal Saturn. Jupiter also entered in Capricorn in March 2020. In September 2020, Rahu was in Taurus and forming a square aspect with his natal Moon. There was also a harsh aspect to Uranus and Neptune.

Suddenly his life started turning negative one after the other and the man who had seen a very good corporate career in the last two decades suddenly lost his job. He ventured into starting his own business but went bankrupt and lost a huge amount of money. He was hospitalized for a few months due to depression. After some time, he was able to overcome all such situations in life and has now become a completely changed person.

Example 5:

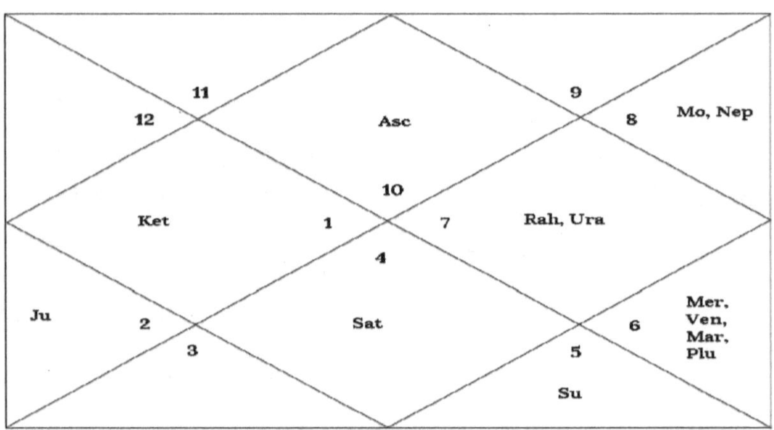

Asc.- Capricorn-18:06:07   Sun-Leo-14:38:42

Moon-Scorpio-5:47:49   Saturn-Cancer-17:14:25

This is another case of the person born in the year August 1976, His Ascendant is Capricorn and natal Saturn is situated in the 7th house. On Jan 2020, transit Saturn was in Ascendant and created square aspect to Ketu, opposition aspect to his natal Saturn and 10th aspect to MC. After that time, matter towards his family, with his wife and his job get highly disturbed. Hard aspects of Uranus and Neptune intensified the matter. He suffers some medical problems due to Jupiter transit in Capricorn, but trine aspect to his natal Jupiter increased his level of creativity.

Example 6:

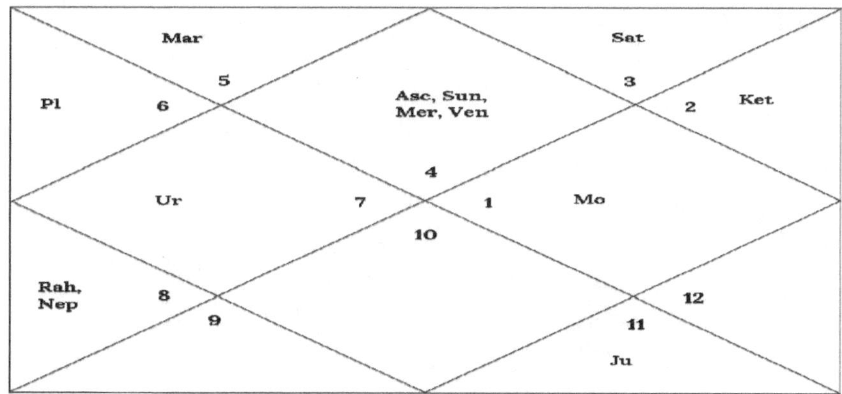

Asc.- Cancer-01:00:07   Sun- Cancer-23:25:40
Moon-Aries-09:09:49   Saturn-Gemini-19:55:18

This is the chart of the person born in the year August 1974. His Sun is in ascendant in Cancer sign, and Moon is in 10th house in Aries. Transit Saturn in Jan. 2020 in Capricorn has created hard aspects with ascendant, Sun and Moon. It was also forming opposition with Mercury and Venus. In such a situation, the matter related to his office worsened during the transit. Saturn has created hard aspect simultaneously with Sun, Moon, Asc. and MC. The person has faced immense pressure to the matter of these houses. The matter starts eases in his life when Saturn enters in Aquarius in April 2023 for a short time, but it has indicated that Saturn's transit in Aquarius will be beneficial for him. At the time of writing the book Saturn is about to enter in Aquarius and all the problems is his life is solved, everything turns in favor. The tension at the workplace is gone and he has become a very favorite employee for his superiors.

Example 7:

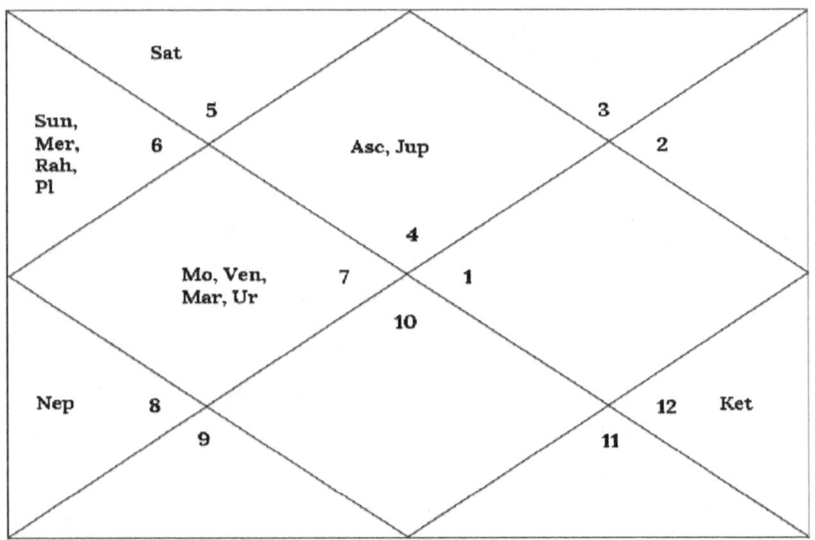

Asc.- Cancer-16:19:07   Sun- Virgo-16:41:29
Moon-Libra-05:21:04   Saturn-Leo-15:00:55

This is the chart of the person born in the year October 1978. His Jupiter in exalted in ascendant. The person has seen a very good corporate career after his education. When Saturn entered in Capricorn it created hard aspects with his ascendant and the

Moon and makes no aspect with his Sun. Other than short problems and tension during such transit nothing else is visible in here.

But presently, the person is running under Mahadasha of Saturn and Venus antardasha started during April 2020. When we explore such a period in our ancient text, Chapter XII, first stanza of Bhavartha Ratnakar states that "When Saturn's dasha, Venus bhukti starts or Venus dasha Saturn bhukti begins, such period is highly unfortunate for the person." Venus is the planet of luxury and comfort and Saturn hates all these things. Saturn is the planet which keeps the person secluded and devoid of all kinds of luxuries and comforts. Saturn teaches hard lesson to the person and shows the harsh truth of life which a person cannot see in his heydays.

The circumstances in his life changed drastically in April 2020 and Uranus forced the person to leave the current path. This person had a great desire to open his own venture but due to some reason he was unable to do that. Now destiny of the person is pulling is a different direction and Uranus is forcing the person to work as per the desire of his soul. Saturn is putting pressure to work hard and with limited resources. During such period exalted Jupiter is providing its protection shield and when Jupiter enters in Pisces which is native's 9th house, it makes trine aspect with the natal Jupiter, such transit increases the native's protection shield. If Jupiter's support was not available, then the situation could have worsened. The destiny of the person is pulling to the next phase of life. Saturn's sign change is indicating easiness in the situation and doors that were closed for almost three years are now opening.

Chapter 7

Astrological Remedies

I have seen in many horoscopes that the transit of two planets plays an important role during midlife crisis – Saturn and Rahu. When such planets start creating hard aspect the person's life does not remain the same as earlier. The impact of these two slow-moving planets is very strong and it creates severe impact on the life of the person. The tough master Saturn starts teaching tough lessons to the person and shows the real picture of the world. The transit of Saturn stays in a sign for 2.5 years and Rahu stays in a sign for 1.5 years. When these two planets start making hard aspect simultaneously, then those years are very difficult years in the life of the person. The cold planet Saturn freezes everything in life and during that period a deadlock-like situation arises in the life of the person.

Simultaneously, the effect of other planets also creates impact. But after some time, when one after another planets start changing their positions momentum again starts in life. But till then the person has seen the both side of the coin.

Following are a few astrological remedies:

7.1 The Sun

When the Sun is weak in a horoscope the native has low self-confidence, is unable to go ahead alone, and always seeks dependency, the problem with the boss, lack of support with father or relation with father is not good, problem in eyes, frustrate very easily and feel depressed, suffer from an inferiority complex, unable to digest the word "No", bone-related problem, tries to hide himself and less socializes, suffer from frequent headaches, always feeling insecure and seeking safety first.

Remedies for the Sun:

- Chant Aditya Hridaya Stotra daily

- Chant Chakshushopanishad for problems related to eyes

- Take the blessing of your mother and father

- Avoid meat and stick to a vegetarian meal

- Never accept any gift for free of cost, except for parents

- Donate dark red colored clothes

- Avoid eating salt on Sunday

- Wear Ruby

7.2 The Moon

Weak Moon in a chart indicates; mental illness, quickly bored and always looking for new excitement, pessimistic thoughts, always finding fault and making a complaint, bad relation with mother, always suspect the activities of spouse or lover, and frequent quarrel with them on any trivial matter, lack of control on mind, being easily attracted to useless items while shopping and making unnecessary purchases, lack of adjustment on new places, easily catch cough and cold, not able to keep any secret in mind and feel an urge to say anyone's matter to others.

Remedies for the Moon:

- Always respect your mother and never argue with her

- Turn off the television, computer, mobile, etc. at least one hour before going to sleep

- Mediate for a few minutes every morning

- Stop water leakage immediately from your house

- Stop passing one person's information to other

- Never discuss confidential things with anyone

- Feed Birds

- Wear Pearl

7.3 Mars

If Mars is weak; frequent cuts and minor wounds are possible, the problem of blood pressure, energy level low in the body, and always feel sleepy, a person easily gets angry and suffers from frequent headaches, ready to quarrel and always seek revenge, the problem of anemia and reproductive organs, females have a problem of abortions, problem-related with land, suffer minor or major accidents while traveling, dispute with siblings, face issues with police and frequent visit of the police station, hide here and there in fear of being caught.

Remedies for Mars:

- Chant Hanuman Chalisa daily

- Recite the Gayatri mantra daily

- Do not quarrel with anyone and do not fight on the streets

- Do not quarrel with siblings and always please them with gifts

- Maintain good relations with your family members and avoid leaving in nuclear families

- Donate blood occasionally

- Stop eating non-veg foods

- Wear Red Coral

7.4 Mercury

Weak mercury indicates; problems in communication, lack of analytical mind, wrong business decisions, low memory and the problem of forgetfulness, weak nervous system, skin-related problems, adolescence-onset sex problems and sex deviance, reduction of sexual strength, lack of focus on study, trying shortcuts in the examination, the problem of jealously with their friends, etc.

Remedies for Mercury:

- Quit alcohol

- Eat green vegetables

- Stop watching worthless movies and TV serials

- Don't argue with your friends and praise them for their success

- Wake up early

- Wear Emerald

7.5 Jupiter

Weak Jupiter indicates; excess fat in the body, lever-related problems, no interest in reading books, problem in education, no interest in religious activities, the problem with teachers, loss of gold, wrong charges of theft, diabetes, childless couple, etc.

Remedies for Jupiter:

- Read Vishnu Sahasranama Sthotram

- Eat turmeric

- Wear gold

- Spread knowledge and help students

- Read good books

- Take blessings for Guru and always respect

- Wear Yellow Sapphire or Pukhraj

7.6 Venus

Weak Venus indicates; beauty-related problems, unusual attraction toward the opposite sex, no support from females, quarrels with females, worthlessly buying fancy items and no control on expenditure, problem-related with reproductive organs, problem in the kidney, interest in pornography, always demanding attention, etc.

Remedies for Venus:

- Worship Lord Durga

- Always wear neat and clean cloths

- Never accept free gifts

- Eat cow ghee

- Do not eat foods with preservatives and chemicals

- Respect mother

- Do not argue with females and always help her

- Wear Diamond

7.7 Saturn

Weak Saturn indicates; problems with labour, pessimistic thoughts, lack of vigor, always looking at the dark side, frequent change of servants and subordinates, disloyal servants, always delay in work and never completing work on time, like to eat cold and stale foods, chronic diseases, etc.

Remedies for Saturn:

- Chant Shani Chalisa

- Always clean nearby surroundings where you live

- Always maintain balance in every situation and avoid overindulgence in any matter of life

- Avoid indulging in any type of court matter

- Donate footwear

- Wear Blue Sapphire

7.8 Rahu

Weak Rahu indicates; One is always afraid of snakes and always looks down to see if there is any snake, fingernails become weak and turn black, indulges in worthless quarrels often, no peace of his mind, and tendency to steal items, etc.

Remedies for Rahu:

- Chant Hanuman Chalisa

- Worship Lord Durga

- Never cheat any person

- Always control your temptation

- Wear Hessonite or Gomeda stone

7.9 Ketu

Weak Ketu indicates; disbelief in religion, always trying to hide the face, diseases by bacteria, headless state of mind, lack of direction, unable to detect diseases easily, untruthful religious leader, etc.

Remedies for Ketu:

- Worship Lord Ganesha

- Do spiritual activities

- Donate blanket

- Feed street dogs and never beat them

- Never take hasty decisions

- Wear Cat's Eye stone

Chapter 8

Turn a Crisis into an Opportunity

Every crisis provides an opportunity. But you have to think out of the box to see the opportunity. The mind which is already following a regular pattern is not ready to accept the sudden changes in life. Because following a daily pattern provides a comfortable zone and it is very difficult for anyone to leave such an area.

But now the crisis has knocked on the door. Now, a change has started in life that takes the person to another part of his journey. The journey is destined by the nature to the person and when the journey is long then more preparation has to be done. Hence, some people overcome such stages in life with zero or few hurdles, because they need not change their tracks, but some have to face difficult stages in life. Here are some tips to help you prepare yourself for such a long journey that turns a crisis into an opportunity.

8.1 Accept the Crisis

When times change, people are not ready to accept it. Situations change rapidly and solutions are difficult. A midlife crisis is teaching them a hard lesson that has never happened before in life. Hence, people are not ready to accept that change as it forces them to come out of their comfort zone. Many people start saying why this is happening in my life, watch others how they are enjoying their lives.

So, first of all, you should accept the change and not compare yourself with others. After your acceptance, your mind will be at peace, and only calm and stress-free mind can take the right decision.

8.2 Stop Blaming Your Luck

I have seen that many people always say – "How unlucky I am". They always blame their luck and compare how lucky others are. When anything happens that they don't like, they start blaming their luck. They are ready to blame their luck on anything they don't like. I've noticed that "Bad Luck" or "How unlucky I am" is a very common word on every other person's tongue.

They feel satisfied after blaming their luck that they found a reason for such incidents in life. Such people get frustrated easily, they are unable to fight adverse circumstances and start crying easily. When anything happens that they don't like, they are ready to say quickly "It is my bad luck".

You must remember that your luck is your Jupiter. When you blame your luck, you are blaming your Jupiter. Such words prohibit you to think constructively. Blaming your luck starts the vicious cycle of your misfortune.

I remember an incident, I was working in an organization, and one day my boss said "Ajay, it is very bad luck that such things happened to you." I replied, "Don't worry, my luck always favors me."

What happens when you blame your luck?

- When you blame your luck, you are also blaming your Jupiter which is the lord of wisdom, wealth and direction, etc.

- When you blame your luck, wisdom will disappear from your life. I have seen that such people buy books but do not read them.

- When you blame your luck, wealth will disappear. I have seen that one who always blames his luck suddenly loses his gold ornaments. Remember, Jupiter represents gold. Every person wants gold, in fact every person wants Jupiter. (I explained this topic further in my book "Jupiter: The Planet of Fortune")

- Jupiter provides direction and such a person lacks direction in life when he blames his luck. They keep wandering here and there. They go in one direction and after some time they change their direction. They start one business and when it is not performing, they start blaming their luck. Without Jupiter, the person will waste his time, energy, and money.

So, you should never blame your luck. It is your Jupiter that provides you direction, wealth and wisdom, etc. Without the grace of Jupiter, a person cannot understand the right direction in his life. Jupiter provides expansion and blaming one's luck will destroy the quality of expansion. Soon, such a person becomes narrow-minded and always confused in any matter of life. Such a person lacks the necessary skills to take decisive decisions in life.

8.3 Change Your Priorities and Goals

As we grow in life, our priorities keep on changing. We work hard to achieve the goals we thought of achieving at a young age. But a mid-life crisis suddenly forces the person to change their priorities, which they find difficult. Because it directly affects his intended goal which the person is not ready to give up.

This type of situation in life creates tension and conflict and one start feeling hopeless in life. The person is not ready to give up the path that he is accustomed to, because the new path has many challenges. But don't be afraid of challenges when the times call for you to change. The planetary energy is forcing you to change, so you must support that energy. Struggling with such energy can create chaos in your life.

Listen to your soul's desire and do only what it asks for. Have faith in yourself and start your journey. Very soon you will find that new doors are opening. When you start supporting energy, it will push you toward your destiny.

When the time demands to change your priorities and goals, it is good to change.

8.4 Avoid to Sit in a Dark Room

When people feel frustrated and depressed, they like to sit in a dark room. Saturn the slow-moving planet brings frustration and depression to life. Saturn teaches tough lessons to the person which the person never forgets in his life. Saturn is also a cold, dark, and farthest planet. Therefore, when the saturnine effect starts surrounding the person, things in life start freezing, and remember that Saturn stays in a sign for 2.5 years.

When Saturn starts testing the patience of the person, he must show his full courage and avoid all gloomy thoughts from his mind. Be ready to learn what Saturn is teaching and the tough master will show you the real picture of the world.

One must follow the following techniques to avoid gloomy situations in life;

- Avoid sitting in a room where the light is off and where sunlight is not coming

- Avoid going in isolation

- Keep all negative thoughts away from your mind

- Socialize with your friends

- Always keep yourself and your surroundings clean

- Utilize your time to develop your hobby

8.5 Take care Your Health

Saturn also represents old age and diseases. During a midlife crisis, I have noticed that not only career-related issue but health-related matter also starts. However, it depends on various types of conjunction in the horoscope and it is not necessary that every person who is suffering from a midlife crisis health-related matter to arise. But it is good to take precautionary steps. Other than taking care of health, change in dietary habits and doing exercise one such step I suggest that it is good to take a reasonable amount of medical insurance.

I remember an incident; I was analyzing a friend's horoscope a few years back and I saw some negative combinations that could affect his health. I suggested to him that it is good for you to take a health insurance. He was surprised to hear my advice as everything was going well in his life and he was promoted that year. I said, if nothing happens then it is very good, otherwise, you will be at least financially secure. He did not listen to my advice and told me that his health is absolutely fine and he has office insurance but I realize that the amount was less. Later, I forgot about that incident.

Two and half years later he called me and said that he had suffered a severe heart attack and had undergone bypass surgery.

The expenses were huge and the office insurance was inadequate.

8.6 Try to Keep Balance

Before Midlife many of us create an imbalance in life regarding our relations, our health, our children, and in many other matters. In some aspects, we focus a lot and in some we ignore. A midlife crisis provides an opportunity to keep balance in every sphere of life and special attention is required on those matters where the level of imbalance is high.

Saturn is the planet of justice that always maintain balance in every sphere of life. Saturn is exalted in libra which symbol is a scale that represents the working of Saturn which do perfect balance if an imbalance exists anywhere. Therefore, it is good to maintain balance to avoid tough lessons from Saturn.

For example, let's say a person has deceived someone and has been able to fool everyone. It is good for him to repent for such an act, otherwise he cannot escape the punishment of Saturn. Learn to keep balance, without which you cannot go ahead in life.

I remember an incident; One day a friend of mine sent me his horoscope and a photo of his injured leg. He told me that he had a serious leg accident yesterday, and asked if you could tell me whether there was any combination of such an accident in my horoscope. I analyzed the chart and saw that his natal Mars and Saturn are aspecting his twelfth house. I asked "do you have a serious ankle injury", he replied "yes", and said "but many others can have such combinations, which means each person's foot will hurt". I replied "no", it is not necessary. Surely, you did something wrong with your foot in past. Then he told me that when he was young, he used to beat students with feet during his college days. I said, now transit Saturn has given you such a punishment and punishment is necessary to strike a balance.

8.7 Change Your Habits

A midlife crisis forces the person to put question whatever he has done till now. If the desire of the soul is different from what he did then great perplexity arises in the mind of the person.

Our thoughts in our subconscious mind matter most than what we say and think in our conscious mind. These thoughts compel the person to change their habits and sometimes the night's sleep is lost due to the intense impulse of thoughts.

For example, suppose a person is not satisfied what he is doing in his life, his soul desires something other and that is deep in his mind. But due to various reasons, he never told this to anyone neither he makes any effort, due to family responsibility, lack of time, or any other reason. But when Uranus starts creating opposition aspect then discrimination starts in his life. His mind functions towards change and those thoughts are very impulsive. The new path suddenly demands many changes in life.

In such times, many people have noticed a change in their habits. They start developing a new skill which was earlier just a seed in their mind. It is possible that a person who drinks a lot of alcohol suddenly starts giving up such a habit. Die-hard non-vegetarians start changing their dietary habits. It is good to support such change because time is demanding and you cannot go ahead with old baggage on your shoulder.

8.8 Focus on Your Strength

Every person has some strengths and weaknesses and people say, overcome your weakness. But I believe that it is better to focus only on your strengths and leave behind your weaknesses. You can move ahead in life only with the power of your strength. Focus only on those weaknesses that are hindering you from strengthening your strengths.

For example, suppose someone is good at singing and poor at mathematics. If he works hard in mathematics then he will not be successful in life because his mind is not working to understand complex mathematical calculations. Rather it is good for him to focus on singing and strengthen this skill so that one day he will become a good singer.

Focus only on your strength and leave behind your weakness. After some time, you will realize that many of your weaknesses have been removed. The problem is that people do not realize what is their strength. They do not work hard to strengthen their strength. They listen to their weakness from others and start working on their improvement.

But by repeatedly hearing about one's weaknesses from others, one becomes forget his strength. Hence, focus only on your strength, the day when your fingers are burned your weaknesses automatically goes away.

8.9 Develop New Skills

The development of new skills is necessary at this juncture of life. As per your inclination, you should develop new skills. Learning is a continuous journey and many people don't learn anything new after leaving college.

If you do not focus on developing your skills then you will not be able to face the challenges in the coming years. The Midlife crisis will not be in your life forever. Soon, time will change, but you will miss out on a great opportunity if you don't focus on your development and just waste time wandering around.

8.10 Take Participation in New Activity

A midlife crisis provides an opportunity for development. So, it is not good to sit idle in one place and think about the past. Thinking about your past will isolate you and make it difficult for you to come out of your gloomy face. So, start participating in new activities, it will help you to change your thoughts. Make new friends and become a volunteer in some activities.

People feel hopeless because they are stuck with their world and they hesitate to explore something new in life because it is risky. But it never happened that all doors closed in life forever. When one door has closed the path for the new door opens. But it requires changing your direction. If you constantly knock on the door that has closed, then you feel frustrated.

Therefore, it is better to participate in a new activity that will bring your enthusiasm back to life.

8.11 Think About Differentiation, But Carefully

During midlife, people think about doing something different in life. In the house Uranus is placed, people always think about doing something different. They keep on changing and are not satisfied with the change. For example, to stand out from others, a person buys a luxury car or any other vehicle or any other product which is not easily available in the market but after some time he feels dissatisfied and starts thinking of changing it.

If Uranus is placed with the Moon or makes an aspect, that person always discusses doing something different in life. They are not very clear about what difference they want, but what others are doing, they don't want to do that. But if Jupiter is aspecting the Moon or Uranus, then the person gets a clear direction in life. Due to the absence of Jupiter, the level of confusion in a person is high. He is always in dilemma and unable to take concrete decisions. Energy needs direction without which it cannot produce any fruitful result. The energy that has the power to produce differentiation may go in vain if the decision is not taken after full consideration.

Uranus is such a fire that produces differentiation. But the power of fire should not be in the hands of a fickle-minded person. It can cause harm to oneself and others and the person may burn all his resources. You cannot undo the difference that fire creates. So, if your energy is forcing you to do something different, go ahead, but do it with caution.

8.12 This is The Time to Sow Seeds

The pace in the life does not remains the same forever. It changes after some time. When days are good, people don't expect that one day it will change. When the life hits the bottom, people work hard to make their activities increase in the outside world. They expect the result soon but when the time takes, they get disappointed very soon. It is necessary to understand the momentum of time in life.

When tailwinds start you can go far with little effort, but when headwinds start, it's better not to waste energy, and wait for the time to come.

You may not always be involved in the activities of the outside world in life. The cycle keeps on changing as day and night. So, when your life hits the bottom, it is good time to sow the seeds for your future. Remember, you can only sow seeds at the bottom. If you want your tree to flourish one day then you will have to dig deep, sow the seeds and take care of your plant for some time.

But no one wants to sow a seed when their life comes to a halt. They want to sow it when everything is shining in their life. Shining means that at this time the air element is favorable in your life, without the help of air element in your horoscope no one can shine. But if you sow the seeds this time it will go in vain, because air does not help in sowing but helps in spreading. But people want the fruits of their seeds soon when they through the seeds on air. They do not know that it will take time for the seed thrown in the air to touch the suitable land and many of never find that ground.

When every activity in your life stops, and you are away from the outside world. Don't feel disheartened when you see the true face of your close and intimate, when your life hits the bottom. Utilize it in the following manner;

- It's Time to Sow the Seeds

- It's Time to Meditate

- It's Time to Introspect Your Life

- It's Time to Learn Something New

The time has come to thank God for providing such an opportunity and such a deep vision that many people do not have. This is the beginning of a new journey of life.

Bibliography

Brihat Parashara Hora Sastra by Maharshi Parasara

Brihat Jatak, Translation by Prof. P.S. Sastri, Rajan Publications, New Delhi

Jatak Parijat, Translation by V. Subramanya Sastri, Rajan Publications, New Delhi

Bhavartha Ratnakar, Translation by B.V. Raman, UBS Publishers, New Delhi,

ABC of Indian Astrology, Prof. (Dr.) Nimai Banerjee, Published by Mrs. Kanti Banerjee, Cuttak

Fundamental Principals of Astrology, by Prof. K.S. Krishnamurti

Fundamentals of Vedic Astrology by Bepin Behari

Myths and Symbols of Vedic Astrology by Bepin Behari

Scientific Hindu Astrology Vol 1 &2 by P.S. Sastri

Sayan 1, by Shard C. Joshi, Bharatiya Vidya Bhavan, Mumbai

Solar system exploration<https://solarsystem.nasa.gov/planets/mars/in-depth/> Accessed on 6th Feb 2022

Welcome to starchild<https://starchild.gsfc.nasa.gov/docs/StarChild/StarChild.html> Accessed on 16th Feb 2022

COSMOS - The SAO Encyclopedia of Astronomy<https://astronomy.swin.edu.au/cosmos/> Accessed on 16th Feb 2022

Swami Vivekananda Quotes<https://quotefancy.com/> Accessed on 17th Feb 2022

About The Author

Ajay Srivastava is the founder of lotuswisdom.in and holds 'Bachelor of Science' from Deen Dayal Upadhyay Gorakhpur University, Gorakhpur (UP) and 'Masters Programme in International Business' from PSG Institute of Management, Coimbatore (Tamil Nadu).

He has extensive experience in the capital market as a Lead Analyst, Investment Banker, Consultant, and Advisor in identifying investment opportunities and formulating strategies. In his career, he has written various research notes and has done in-depth research from a commercial and financing point of view in multiple deals. With diverse industry experience and wide understanding, he started imparting his knowledge in the industry since 2013.

He has deep knowledge of graphology and since childhood he is very much interested in analyzing a person by handwriting and has analyzed the handwriting of hundreds of persons in his life.

He is very much passionate to learn about astrology in deep and has completed a Five-years Course - ' JyotirVisharada ' in Astrology from Bharatiya Vidya Bhavan, Mumbai.

Email ID: ajay.srivastava@lotuswisdom.in

Web Site: http://www.lotuswisdom.in/

Books Written by the Author

1. Psychology and Investment

2. Vedic Astrology: The Light of Wisdom

3. Midlife Crisis: An Astrological Appraoch

4. Jupiter: The Planet of Fortune

5. The Joy of Creation and Success

6. The Light of Nakshatras

7. Sun: The Supreme Creator

8. Astrology & Predictions

9. Animal Symbols of Nakshatras

10. Astrology & Profession (Coming Soon)

Astrology Courses

1. Nakshatra Course

Knowledge of Nakshatra is very important in astrology, without it one cannot understand how energy works and what will be the result of the transit of planets. Do not limit yourself to the movement of planets, explore the world of Nakshatra and understand the hidden secrets.

What You'll Learn

• How the knowledge of Nakshatra helps to understand the characteristics and negative traits of the person

• Effect of transit of planets and time of activation

• Meaning of each symbol and its influence

• Influence of the associated animal on the personality of the person

• When to start a new venture and when not to go ahead

• Related Profession

• Understand each concept with logic

Course Offerings:

• 54 hours of live sessions (2 hours each Nakshatra)

• Learn various astrological concepts with practical examples

• Mode – Online Classes, Recordings available;

• Medium – English

Contact Us:

Mobile No.: +91 9867837184

Email ID: ajay.srivastava@lotuswisdom.in

Visit my blog for registration:

https://lotuswisdomonline.blogspot.com/

2. <u>Vedic Astrology for Beginners {Level – 1 (Basics)}</u>

Module – 1: Basics of Astrology

Introduction; The Zodiac; Elements

Module – 2: Signs

Meaning of the Signs, Elements of the Signs, Qualities of the Signs, Odd and Even Signs, Sheershodaya & Prishtodaya Signs, Direction, Colors, Caste, Fruitful and Barren Signs, Masculine & Feminine Signs, Places, Other Major Qualities

Module – 3: Houses

Meaning of the 12 Houses, Types and Classifications of Houses

Module – 4: Planets

Planets and their Characteristics, Planetary Relationship, Exaltation, Debilitation & Mooltrikona, Natural Karakas, Karakas in Jaimini Astrology

Module – 5: Planets in Groups

Natural Benefic and Malefic Planets, Gender; Color; Caste; Guna and Places; Planet and Tastes; Nature of Planet; Elements; Metals; Age; Cloth and Height; Vegetable and Fruits; Physical Constituents and Tendency; Maturity Age of Planets; Planetary Aspects; Seasons

Module – 6: Planetary Strengths and Weaknesses

Strength of Planets based on its degrees, Direction; Direction Strength; Maran Karaka Sthana; Yog Karaka; Vargottam Planet; Shadabala

Module – 7: Retrograde and Combust Planet, Gandanta

3. <u>Vedic Astrology for Beginners {Level – 2 (Advanced)}</u>

Module 1: Vimshottari Dasha System

Nakshatra and Planetary Lordship, Change of Dasa and Results

Module 2: Basics of Nakshatra

Deity, Animal Symbol, Caste, Activity, Gana, Guna, Gender

Module 3: Important Yogas

Know the 30 most important astrological combinations

Module 4: Ashtakvarga

Interpretation of Ashtakvarga Table

Module 5: Transit of Planets and their impact

Understand the effect of transit of Jupiter, Saturn, Rahu-Ketu

Module 6: Planets and Profession

Identify the influence of the planet and the direction of profession

Module 7: Weak Planets and Remedies

Identify the signal of weak planets and useful remedies

Module 8: Key Steps to Chart Interpretation

Course Offerings:

· 30 hours of live sessions (Level 1 & Level 2)

· Learn various astrological concepts with practical examples

· Mode - Online Classes

· Recordings available

· Medium - English

Contact Us:

· Mobile No.: +91 9867837184

· Email ID: ajay.srivastava@lotuswisdom.in

Visit my blog for registration:

https://lotuswisdomonline.blogspot.com/

PSYCHOLOGY
AND
INVESTMENT
The Art of Investing in Stocks with an
Explanation of Human Psychology
AJAY SRIVASTAVA

The Joy
of
Creation and Success
Ajay Srivastava

Midlife
Crisis: An
Astrological
Approach
Understand The Timing Of Crisis,
Learn How To Turn A Crisis Into An Opportunity
Ajay Srivastava

Astrology
&
Predictions
Ajay Srivastava

Author's Page